John Gonta, MA, MS, Jd
Attorney at Law
Monroe, Michigan 48161

Wow, here is a book that will open your mind!

By going through the "9 Golden Rules" we are taken on a journey through the "journey of life . . ." What a good concept. The book shows how to take control of your life, which is stated as Golden Rule #1. It is great to read a book that helps the reader grasp the simple concepts of life as a journey and how to take hold of that journey and make it benefit the reader.

I suggest this book to many of my clients as not only good reading but also to heal them through trying times. I've been an attorney in the State of Michigan for over 22 years and this is by far the best reading I have encountered.

Thanks,
John Gonta

The Golden Rules
of a
Successful
Breakthrough

CHRISTIAN MILLIONAIRE
Steven Lawrence Hill Sr

ASA PUBLISHING CORPORATION

AN INNOVATIVE OUTSOURCE BOOK PUBLISHING HYBRID

ASA Publishing Corporation
1285 N. Telegraph Rd., PMB #376, Monroe, Michigan 48162
An Accredited Publishing House with the BBB
www.asapublishingcorporation.com

BBB
100 YEARS
Advancing Trust Together

Copyrights © 2020 Steven Lawrence Hill Sr., All Rights Reserved ®

Book Title: The Golden Rules of a Successful Breakthrough

Date Published: 01.17.2020 / Edition 1 *Trade Paperback*

Book ID: ASAPCID2380799

ISBN: 978-1-946746-70-2

LCCN: Cataloging-in-Publication Data

This book was published in the United States of America.

Great State of Michigan

Table of Contents

Introduction

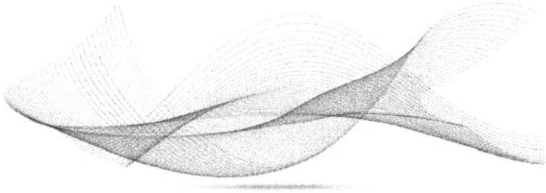

It's not about the person, place, or thing that is in front of you, it's about you facing up against yourself and the courage to make the right decisions that allows you to make a choice of what kind of people, places, and things that you want to involve yourself with.

In order to do that, we need to discover how did things get so out of control in our lives and what can we do to restore a positive balance with these golden rules inside of the three elements that make up our world.

Together we (you) will learn so much more about Ourselves, Our Personal Environment, and Our Environmental Surroundings, and how toxic it can become if we do not have positive control over them.

Just like a resolution, the first thing we need to do is to take a positive step in making a covenant within our own selves, knowing that from this point on, we (you) are commited to wanting a positive change in your life.

Covenant Pledge

The core is me. All that I am is within the way I think. I am the product of myself. Therefore, if God has given me the free will to choose, then the choices that I make is within the way I am thinking. Then it is I, myself, who chooses to either be broken by negativity, or allow positivity to uplift my spirits.

I must understand that by allowing the absorption of my thinking, I have opened the door for it to be consumed, replaced, repaired or damaged, piled on or removed, of whatever it is that I was thinking or dwelling on at that time. The choice I make concerning whether to accept or reject the absorption, it is within my power to control.

If my thoughts are becoming, has been, or beginning to become unstable, then I need to discover and address what it is that hinders the pathway of positive thinking in my life, and replaces it with the poor choices that I continue to make and/or create for myself. The first thing I need to do, is to take back control of my life.

My name is _____ and this is my Covenant Pledge commitment to God and myself to begin taking back control of my life on this _____ day in the month of _____, within this year _____.

Congratulations! You just had your first breakthrough, now it's time to work out your success!

Did You Know?

Lifestyle is all mental.

Once you understand that, then you can move forward from certain preventable situations, the drowning of poverty, the self-afflicting addiction[s], abusive circumstances, and any other problems that you just can't handle at this present time. The only true hard work is convincing yourself to . . .

. . . do what is right.

Reprocessing Our Thoughts Correctly

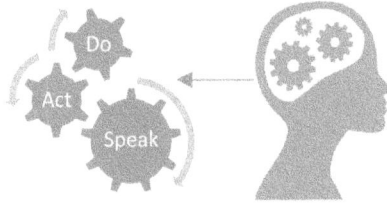

What we feel within our heart is a condition that is placed on a mindset; a mental thought processing by the way on which we think. Therefore, all processing has a core which absorbs negative or positive knowledge. Whether suggestions, influences, directions or instructions, we ourselves are the decision makers on what we mentally eat.

We can consume by visual, verbal, and/or physical absorption. This absorption is a heart traveling mechanism from the stimuli (a response) of the brain on how one reacts, feels; emotions. Mental derailment is a source of lost willpower; the deterioration of the mind and/or self-control.

Then to empower or re-empower into positive thinking, we must first embrace the pattern of our thoughts by learning the ability of Coherent Consciousness, which simply means "to place together a positive thought process."

- Coherent *means* logically connected and intelligible.
- Consciousness *means* awareness, the totality of one's thoughts and feelings.

What is Coherent Consciousness?

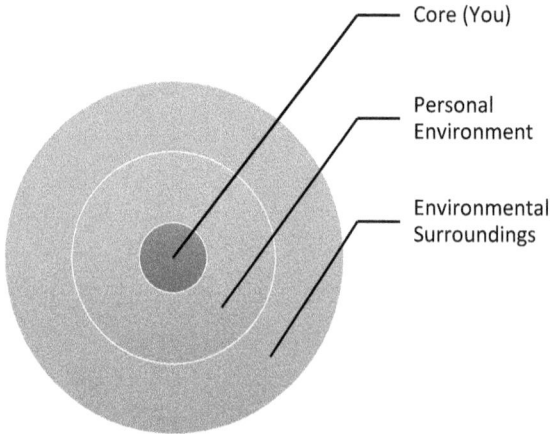

Core (You)

Personal
Environment

Environmental
Surroundings

"**Coherent Consciousness**," is being able to place together a "Positive Thought Process." In learning the ability of "Coherent Consciousness," we must be able to 'activate our minds to a more positive direction' in order to connect our "positive thought patterns" to and with "a positive personal controlled environment." If we do not have control over our own "personal environment," then we cannot regulate "the positive stability" that is needed to reach goals, a destiny, and the ability to maintain focus, as long as the fluctuations of negative and positive forces that creates certain type structures continue to unbalance the production of positive constructiveness, and leaves a trail mark of negative destructive spiritual virus patterns that fleshly manifests and surrounds the outer ring of your core.

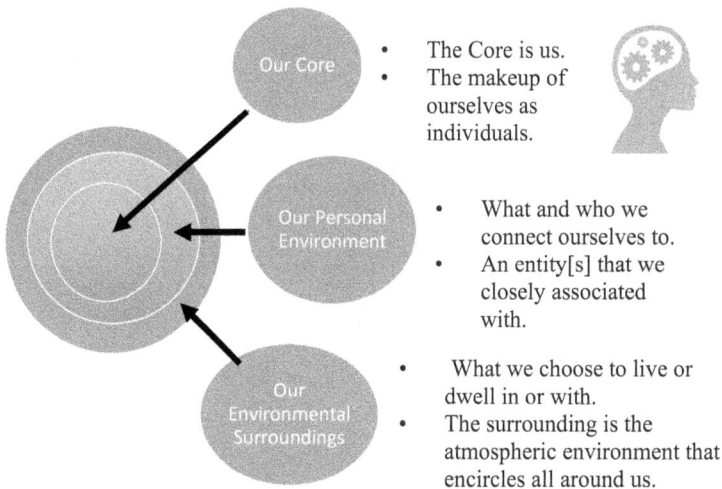

- Our Core
  - The Core is us.
  - The makeup of ourselves as individuals.

- Our Personal Environment
  - What and who we connect ourselves to.
  - An entity[s] that we closely associated with.

- Our Environmental Surroundings
  - What we choose to live or dwell in or with.
  - The surrounding is the atmospheric environment that encircles all around us.

The blueprint of your personal environment would place "you" as the "Core," the outer ring of that core would be your "Personal Environment," which is encircled by your "Environmental Surroundings".

In order to create a positive environment for ourselves, we need to first look at the present personal environment that we have surrounded ourselves with. And in doing so, we can determine just how much negative and/or positive influences of people, places and/or things that grafts our personal environmental makeup. And to obtain a personal controlled environment, we must learn how to be in control of our daily movement in life in order to become successful and/or maintain the success, once it's in our grasp. We will also learn about the differences in environments that we surround ourselves with, and how it can and/or could affect our destiny and/or our goals within the realms of negativity, as well as the realms of positivity.

What is Coherent Consciousness about?

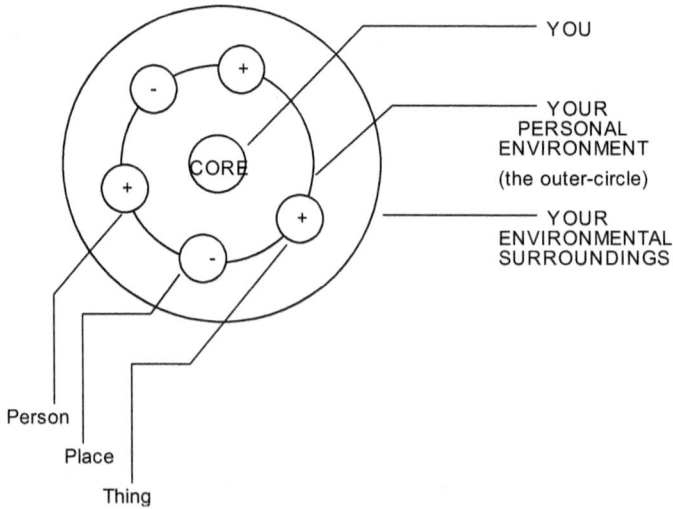

YOU

YOUR
PERSONAL
ENVIRONMENT
(the outer-circle)

YOUR
ENVIRONMENTAL
SURROUNDINGS

CORE

Person

Place

Thing

Providing 'Mental Solutions' to be "Successful and Confident" from any level of society. It is up to you if you want to learn how to overcome certain stressful negativity that takes a hold of your own personal world, because God wants to bless you, "Emotionally, Mentally, Spiritually, Physically, and Financially."

Negativity can be a psychological entity that can cause various symptoms of depression in which can dictate our thoughts to perform verbal or unintentional actions.

There are 9 Golden Rules that we must place within ourselves in order to comprehend what must be done to extract negativity, and apply positive to positive, while becoming positive.

Now it's time to provide you with them!

The Golden Rules
of a
Successful
Breakthrough

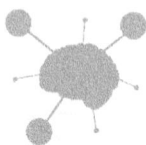

Golden Rule #1
I need to take control of my life

Golden Rule #2
I do not need to explain myself to anyone

Golden Rule #3
I will not allow my past to be used against me, instead I will learn from it, in order to grow

Golden Rule #4
I will learn to be in control of my destiny, and that means avoiding the "time robbers, the controllers, and negative people"

Golden Rule #5
I will not take anymore "mental abuse, physical abuse, and especially spiritual abuse"

Golden Rule #6
I will learn to think before I act

Golden Rule #7
I will learn to think before I speak

Golden Rule #8
I will learn to think before I do

Golden Rule #9
For my "New Life" awaits me!

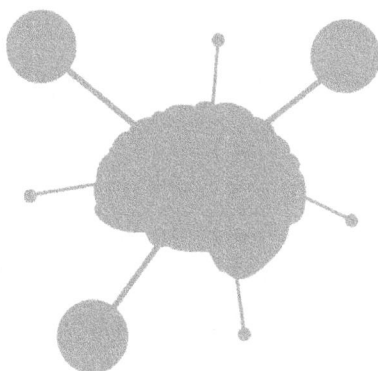

GOLDEN RULE 1

I Need to Take Control of My Life

Have you ever felt like your life is running on its own and/or being ran over? Then there is a chance that this golden rule has been broken by either you and/or violated by allowing a person, place, or thing to start some type of transition to "Demote, Degrade, Demoralize, and/or Deposition" your area of "Coherent Consciousness" as a person who is not and/or have lost their ability of being aware of one's own thoughts and feelings. You have been and/or causing yourself to be robbed mentally.

- **Demote** means to reduce to a lower rank.
- **Degrade** means to demote and/or lower in quality, moral character, dignity, debase, and dishonor.
- **Demoralize** means to lower the morale of, to throw into confusion.

- **Deposition** in relation to this golden rule; means to remove someone from a higher position; depose. And "depose" means to "degrade."

Therefore, there is and/or have been a position that have or going to be overthrown in order to place you into one of the four "D" characteristics of their elemental environment. In other words; you just have entered and/or are remaining stagnated in their world and have or had lost control. That means, whatever position I was in or supposed to be in, has been removed or taken away from me.

Just like if I was a parent, for example, and have one of those mates that likes to treat me like trash, then after a while the child or children will detect this and becomes involved. Now my mate did not accept what I had to say and places me in a position that can make me not stand up for myself. Therefore, the child or children can detect that some part of dignity has been stripped away from me. Then I begin to feel its presence as well through the eyes and heart of those of my surroundings.

By understanding this example, it demonstrates that a "D" element has pulled this individual into its world, and there this individual will remain feeling trapped and withered.

Golden Rule #1 is plain and simple to remember: I need to take control of my life!

Other "D" elements can easily pull a person in just by the obsession of money; causing them to spend and/or neglect their obligations. Others, letting pride go to their head; by trying to feel like they have to make a point that they have become better than the next person; only to find out that they have lost control from positive thinking through the lack of humility. Then there are those who loves to hang around with negative people and wonder why they are always feeling down on themselves. And/or just by allowing these same type of people gain authority; or shall we say control, by allowing their negative selves to feel a power of confidence at the expense of other's misery. Then you got those who thrive on running other's lives. These are what you call "the controllers."

And, another way to be pulled in, you have to avoid the "time robbers." These are entities that find a way to extract positive time, and replace them with negative time. To make it plain and simple, time that you needed when you were supposed to be somewhere or doing something, or just trying to get some sleep and now you overslept.

Now either you missed what you were supposed to be doing, and/or you have just lost control of the time that you once had, and/or trying to find a way to make or recreate a new time schedule that wasn't meant for that day.

Remember the old saying, "time is money?" Try that on for size, if you lost control of time and an open window of a blessed opportunity had allowed someone else to receive it when it saw you taking a detour, because you allowed the time that you thought you had to be robbed by someone or some 'thing' that has a very strong distracting hold on you mentally.

A QUESTION TO ASK OURSELVES

"What does it mean to me to take control of my life?"

NOTE:

In this question, never allow ourselves to reflect the word "YOU," because it is easy to misdirect a situation in the opposite direction, then it is to reflect oneself into a verbal mirror.

When we answer this question, we must be able to refer to ourselves as the key term "self-awareness" is for us to use the word "ME," which places ourselves in our own psychological and mental backyard. This is where through the course of these "9 Golden Rules" to wanting a successful living, places that "self-awareness of understandability" within ourselves in order to comprehend the learning process of ourselves as the core, our personal environment, and our environmental surroundings.

At this first stage of the golden rules, we might not be aware of the environments that we have placed ourselves in and/or condition ourselves in. Therefore, by examining certain words like "transition" and "stagnation" before going into the next following sentence or paragraph, these words can also be useful tools to remove mental blockage that we often allow ourselves not to see, which we blind ourselves from the bare-knuckle truth.

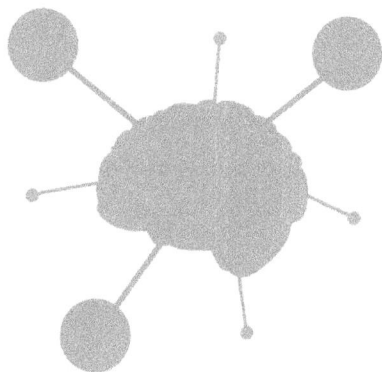

GOLDEN RULE 2

I Do Not Need to Explain Myself to Anyone

The best freedom that anyone can have is "Mental Freedom." Mental freedom can open doors to spiritual freedom, physical freedom, financial freedom and the elimination of the emotional actions that we apply when it seems like there is no results to freedom.

When we have to explain our actions; whether good or bad, what we are doing is not accepting the consequences and/or responsibility that is or has been being brought to our attention. It is as if once we start to give an explanation, there is always someone or some-thing trying to probe us for additional questionnaires. Then comes the *excessive conversations, that has* _extracted unnecessary information_ that was kept between you and the peace of mind that you once had. The icky feeling of whether or not you explained yourself clearly enough, or whether you over explained yourself, and within that itself, you are becoming unsure of whether you have done more harm than good to yourself.

- This is what we call **"Mental Poverty."**
- Mental Poverty produces **"Poor Choices."**
- Poor Choices are based upon our **"Feelings and Emotions."**
- Mental Poverty = **Distractions + Discouragement.** The more the distractions and the more of the discouragements that you obtain, then it becomes the more of poor choices that you will make.

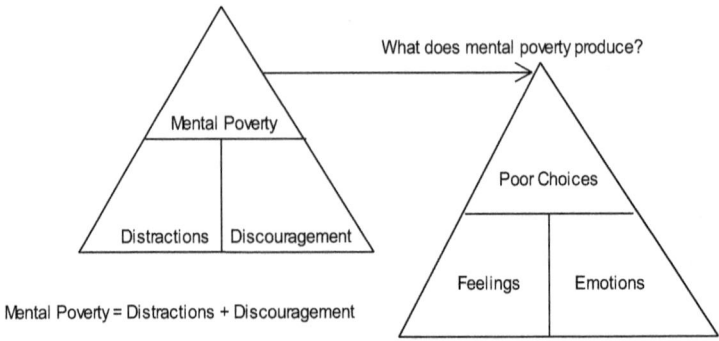

Poor Choices is based upon your "Feelings and Emotions"

You see, God wants to bless you "Emotionally, Mentally, Spiritually, Physically, and Financially." Remember, we are talking about wanting "mental freedom," and in order for this to happen, we have to focus on our own actions. Whether it is verbal and/or physical, we can often project something we didn't want to come into our lives just by our body jesters as another form of a physical attribute to our actions.

Of course, there are common replies to general explanations in order to answer a request that was given. But not to answer explanations that opposes a threat to losing your mind over because you are allowing yourself to be mentally violated. This can cause an emotional conflict between you and the spiritual man inside of you, that causes you to mentally set aside spiritual discernment by means of the growth through biblical scriptures, and cause you to act outside of a closeness towards a true Christianic Perfection, on which Christ has been a demonstrating example of the greatest achievement, of what it is like to be humble through "Character Pressure."

Look at him ease dropping to get more dirt on her.

Boy-o-boy! They're pulling out more information than a used car salesman.

STOP LOSING YOUR MIND . . . IT'S DONE, NOW GET OVER IT!

Ephesians 4:26 and 27 says to "Be ye angry, and sin not: let not the sun go down upon your wrath. Neither give place to the devil." But we know that there is a distance that we need to learn between that scripture and the scripture in Psalms 37:37 which says, "Mark the perfect man, and behold the upright: for the end of that man is peace." And that means, combining "love and humility" with boldness!

Don't let people use car salesman techniques to extract [*fishing out*] information to get to you. If you feel the intensity of pressure invading your mental capacity to comprehend, be careful not to extend that pressure into spilling over into your emotional actions. Because before you know it, you just blown a good fruit out the fruit basket in Galatians 5:22 and 23, and picked up some type of unnecessary garbage out of Galatians 5:19, 20, and 21, just to destroy the testimony of someone or yourself who is looking forward in the continuation of an inheritance in the Kingdom of God.

For the Kingdom of God is still within you, but as they say, "actions speak louder than words." And if someone or some 'thing' can get you to act out of character by "character pressure," then you have allowed yourself to become unintentionally distracted, and soon followed by a discouragement in order to perform the poor choices that you really didn't intend to make and/or create for yourself. Again, "Mental Poverty," which is based upon our

"Feelings" and our "Emotions."

Example: *If your emotional state clouds your judgment, then you cannot think properly. Therefore, your mental comprehension will not allow the spiritual man within you to grow to a level of maturity.*

Whether you have accepted God or a higher power at some point in your life, it doesn't matter because you cannot hear, nor see the signs unless you chose to ignore them by dimming the 'mental lights of awareness' in your noodle. Prayer is good, but it is of no effect if the answer has fallen upon a def ear.

But what does matter at this moment in time is that you 'refocus' on what is happening to you and/or around you that is causing you to mentally imbalance a positive way of thinking, and causing you to make those poor choices that becomes very disabling. The downside is that a person, a place, or a thing acting like Dracula can capitalize on this frailty and do the thinking for you.

What is Dracula?

Dracula is a negative entity that has only one purpose in life, and that is to suck the life out of you or turn you into a zombie to do its bidding.

In other words, negative people, places, or things can cause you to think that you lost all hope or become a dominating controller over you. Leaving you in despair.

You have a world of your own that you can control (Examine Blueprint below). It's when you have a Dracula coming into your world *by invitation only*, and offers you appealing appetites of friendship, a codependency to whatever your desire is, and a trip to the cemetery to see the pretty flowers.

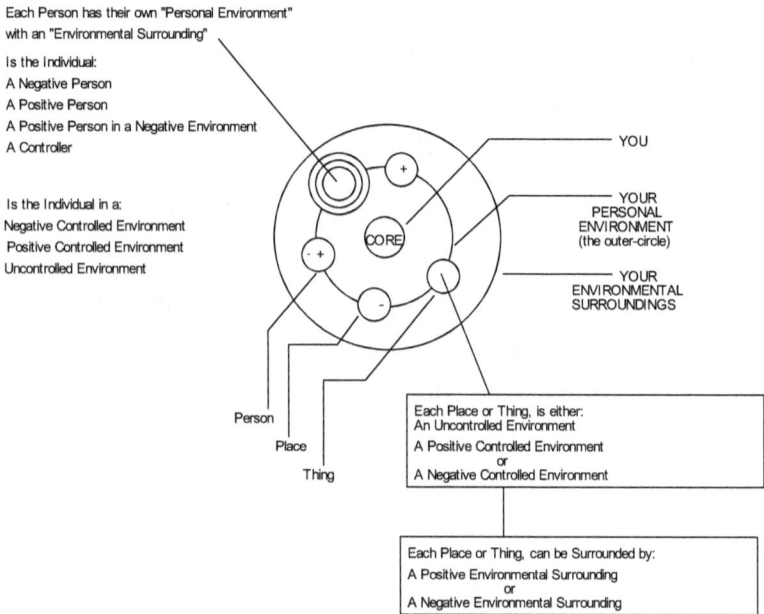

Each Person has their own "Personal Environment" with an "Environmental Surrounding"

Is the Individual:
A Negative Person
A Positive Person
A Positive Person in a Negative Environment
A Controller

Is the Individual in a:
Negative Controlled Environment
Positive Controlled Environment
Uncontrolled Environment

CORE

YOU

YOUR PERSONAL ENVIRONMENT (the outer-circle)

YOUR ENVIRONMENTAL SURROUNDINGS

Person

Place

Thing

Each Place or Thing, is either:
An Uncontrolled Environment
A Positive Controlled Environment
or
A Negative Controlled Environment

Each Place or Thing, can be Surrounded by:
A Positive Environmental Surrounding
or
A Negative Environmental Surrounding

This blueprint that you are examining is your world mapped out in plain view in order for you to understand how you can achieve positive stability.

> This is my world. There are people, places, and things in it that I associate with. But I just can't seem to understand why I'm not in total control of my life.

> Hey you up there! I have a world too. Can I come into your world with skeletons in my closet? I'll tell you later about them. But first, let's get to know each other. I'll even let you ramble on first!

Be careful who you let into your life, if you have not already done so. You are the 'Core' of your world; the center of focus. You can create a better world for yourself, or you can let Dracula continue this one-way ticket courtship in disparage.

> I am the core, the central part of my life. I will learn what it is to have 'positive success' by surrounding myself with positive people, go to positive places, and be able to do positive things, and how to detect the Dracula's and distance myself from them, period!

And how many of us know that our physical appearance plays an important role in our financial growth? You can be the best dressed bum and no-one will ever know that you don't even have a dime in your pocket; it's all about presentation. But having a good presentation about yourself comes with having a positive motivational way of thinking, not excessive chattering.

If someone has the courage to wear their pants below their butt in public, then you should have that same courage to want to elevate yourself from your current situation.

Again, it's in the way you think!

Why are you asking me so many questions? You don't own anything in my world, and I'm not acquiring for a job from you... And by the way, this is the part where I walk out of a senseless conversation!

Never stay in one, nor hang around for unwanted gossip, especially if it's about the conversation that just came out of your mouth. Let the flames burn out of fuel.

So, if you find yourself in an entrapment of excessive unnecessary communicational confrontations, nip it in the bud, take a deep breath, and ask yourself, "Hum . . . , is this type of conversation benefiting me or is it playing with my emotions, because if my feelings are mentally tampered with, then I'm leaving my mind unguarded."

DEFINING WHAT WE LEARNED
SO FAR

We need to understand that sometimes we can say more than what we were intentionally meant to provide, and this can cause a chain reaction to a volunteer probing from the listener. But, this doesn't give the listener the right to extract information to produce some kind of emotional, mental, spiritual, physical, and/or financial harm to the individual [s] unless it is in another process of involvement that places another individual [s] in the hands of a legal authoritative "need to say basis" of information.

"Character Pressure" is pressure that tries to make changes in a person's character [personality] or character traits; to change the quality about a person, or the identity of such an individual that is feeling so much intensity, that the individual loses "self."

"Love and Humility" has two doors that you can go through or come out of. One can be by the means of "boldness," and the other can be by the means of being "timid." Timid is the lacking of courage, the lacking of self-confidence, the lacking in boldness, and/or the lacking of determination [Webster's Collegiate Dictionary].

Therefore, love and humility can be secretly replaced by a timid nature and forced openly to be displayed within its substitution as one who has their love and humility confused with the frailty aspects of their life. Boldness; in relative, is the ability to stand firm without wavering their submissiveness to the ability by which it is well respected and admired, for the grace of love and humility in becoming a humble individual.

Which One's Were in Your Noodle Before?

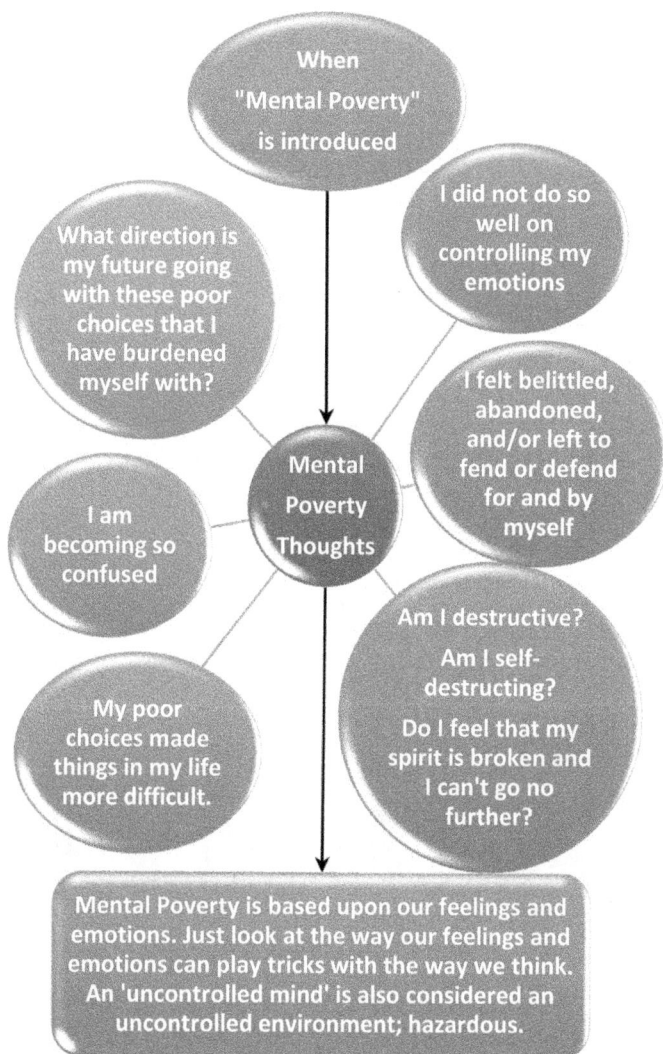

When "Mental Poverty" is introduced

What direction is my future going with these poor choices that I have burdened myself with?

I did not do so well on controlling my emotions

I felt belittled, abandoned, and/or left to fend or defend for and by myself

Mental Poverty Thoughts

I am becoming so confused

Am I destructive? Am I self-destructing? Do I feel that my spirit is broken and I can't go no further?

My poor choices made things in my life more difficult.

Mental Poverty is based upon our feelings and emotions. Just look at the way our feelings and emotions can play tricks with the way we think. An 'uncontrolled mind' is also considered an uncontrolled environment; hazardous.

GOLDEN RULE 3

I will not allow my past to be used against me, instead I will learn from it in order to grow.

Our past can determine the outcome of our future if we allow the historical events of our past lives which carries the destructive side to become the focal point in a *"powerless behavioral pattern,"* when in present, our current situation calls for assistance and/or repair, and not damage control because we have allowed a "spiritual negative force" to become resurrected.

Events like the resurrecting of a spiritual negative force can easily be explained by the term of "bad spirits" in the mist, or better yet, "unclean spirits" of a newer order of evil that has a job of purpose, and that is to await for a command from whomever is at the throne of certain authoritative words that can manipulate an emotional transformation which could place oneself in an internal secret vault, and never release nor transform into a spiritual testimonial messenger that can truly carry words of exhortational spiritual power to the ears and hearts of those who has the same or similar situations, criteria's, and/or addictions that compels an individual to cling onto, or grab a hold of, whether it is a person, place, and/or a thing.

But never the less, these very same individuals have cornered themselves and placed their mental ability in a position of captivity which brings their outward physical lifestyle to be held at bay, due to an event from a past and former life that has now been recalled and exploited through mere verbal words that was brought up to a usage of only providing either shame and/or destruction, as the words continue to gain authority.

We are not threatened by conventional words of hearsay, but we do become petrified when hearsay can bring spiritual death when we do not separate ourselves from those who continue to present mysterious un-acclaimed motives as to why he/she or they must barbwire our thoughts to the point that we cannot function within our range of tolerance, due to over exploded exposure of a past that we wish not to remember.

Then, this brings us back to this newer unclean spirit that is awaiting for its command because it needs a "keyword" to begin its activation. And once it's activated, it will then probe the individual, searching and seeking a way to reactivate as much of the past former demons as it can that was previously shielded through "positive past testimonial breakthroughs."

Although the bible says that we do not war against flesh and blood, but it is in fact a spiritual warfare that we are dealing with. We just have to become more careful by observing to see where these words that surfaces from the past are streamlining from.

Then, there is the "memory." The memory that can be used as a tool which can be a benefit or a hindrance if one so chooses to define what is needed in order to grow or to remain depressed, and/or in a stagnated position.

Whenever the past is brought up into one's present, there are certain strands of a recollection of memories that are attached along with its events that can be utilized in a character growth process of oneself. A character flaw, so to speak, if it is not constructed in a positive way for edifying, repairing, and/or cleared of the conditions that it was brought into for explanations. Because it has a tendency to drive out the true emotional state of an individual through a person's "limited mental stress capacity." In other words; "How much more can a person take having their past thrown up into their face and not being able to defend themselves without accidentally adding additional excuses to their defense?" Then this makes you wonder, if God can forget our past and then throw it in the sea of forgetfulness, why allow the spiritual demonic attacks to prey upon something that is supposed to be forgotten.

Therefore, it is us who reminisce at the instant something is brought up, or better yet, unprotect ourselves from the past when we frequently misread the individuals in whom we have exposed our past to, and bearing our hearts into their trust, including those that we have departed from in the aspect of the neutral, to the almost knuckle bearing unfriendly terms.

So, it is no more than a mere transfer from our unsolved actions that we placed in the fumbling hands of those who are receptive to feed and focus on our frailties (*prey would be the better term*), if we do not understand where will the next domino tumble on; whether it will be on a job, relationship, or good ole' fashion trouble that is awaiting to be stirred up, especially when you least expect it.

Have you ever heard of the expression, "whatever doesn't kill you makes you stronger?" Well, consider becoming stronger by recognizing who it is coming from, where it is coming from, and why it is being presented in a negative fashion. And in that way, recognizing it as a "spiritual negative tactic," you can avoid its manifestation into the fleshly creativity, that wants to separate your spiritual connection with the Third Deity; the Holy Spirit, and falsely imprison your character, as being portrayed as an individual who is still living a remorseful and regretful past, that lingers into the present, only to torture and sere one's mind into "stagnation."

THE "THIRD DEITY" IS THE "HOLY SPIRIT"

The third person of the Trinity, who exercises the power of the Father and the Son in creation and **redemption**. Because the Holy Spirit is the power by which believers come to Christ and see with new eyes of faith, He is closer to us than we are to ourselves. Like the eyes of the body through which we see physical things, He seldom in focus to be seen directly because He is the one through whom all else is seen in a new light.

Redemption: the act, process, or an instance of redeeming.
- Redemption [to "Redeem"]
- To buy back: repurchase
- To free from what distresses or harms
- To free from captivity by payment of ransom
- To extricate from or help to overcome something detrimental
- To free from consequences of sin
- To change for the better: Reform
- To Repair
- To Restore
- To offset the bad effect
- To make worthwhile
- To make good

In "Truly accepting Jesus Christ" as your "Personal Savior" you have already received the Holy Spirit as promised by Him, from God. Therefore, you have been given the "Redemption" that is to be empowered (*given official or legal authority*) by the Holy Spirit Himself, to provide you with the restoration (*restoring you from your situation, circumstance, and/or addiction*).

"Redemption" may be a small gift to receive, but major enough to thank God for! That is why it is so vital to remain connected to God and not disconnected from Christ.

- A reconnection can restore "Redemption Power!"

References: -*Nelson's New Illustrated Bible Dictionary*
-*Webster's Ninth New Collegiate Dictionary*

My mind is a vessel and I am requesting the Holy Spirit's Redemption Power to give my mind the freedom to think clearly.

DON'T WASTE YOUR MIND LETTING SOMETHING RENT ROOM IN THERE

Becoming stronger can also produce growth, and the production of growth increases your limited stress ability to a more tolerant level where your spiritual and mental capability can connect in order to not only give you peace of mind, but stability in positive thinking.

Therefore, one can only gather what information that was presented to them in order to crush one's spirit that can produce the poor choices that we make through a 'poverty state of mind'.

> I sure didn't expect them to use the testimony of her past life to cause her and her fiancé to break off the wedding.

A "Powerless Behavioral Pattern" Is a pattern that is without self-control, which repeatedly loses the self-control in which it supposedly were to obtain, but lacks.

For Example:

When everything is calm, no problem. An individual goes on his/her/their daily life in their normal fashion, as normal is perceived in them. But, if there is a disruption of their "perceived normal flow of things," almost immediately, he/she/they begin to lose self-control.

Therefore, it does not matter how much assistance an individual will receive, nor the amount of repair to restore that which was almost destroyed. But when damage control is called in to rectify [to correct by removing errors and/or adjust] the effects from the destructiveness from losing one's self-control which constantly runs in a repetitious manner, then in the spiritual realm, we in reality, gives open windows of opportunity for new strategies of evil spirits [demons] to find new ways to repetitiously keep us mentally dismantled, whether it involves an affiliation and/or an association with a person, a place, and/or a thing.

And as we read on, this will also explain what is meant by the phrase "a new order of evil" which can be demonstrated by an easy form of verbal power which commands the negative forces that we do not physically see, but destructively powerful in existence, and that is "the negative usage of words."

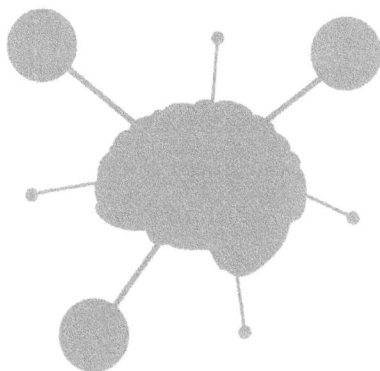

GOLDEN RULE 4

I will learn to be in control of my destiny, and that means avoiding the "Time Robbers", "The Controllers", and "Negative People.".

In everyday life, there is always a "destiny" to reach and/or fulfill, whether to be at a job site on time, to whether searching for a prominent future reaching towards a goal in life itself. However the case may be, it is a destiny that we are trying to maintain some type of achievement; a goal to accomplish.

But, whenever the opposed arrival of this destination has been tampered with, or shall we say, "a flow of resistance" that changes the pattern and/or timeline to be reached, we are no longer in control but puppets of a "negative controlled environment."

Usually a negative controlled environment is actually an "uncontrolled environment." An environment that deals with "time consumption" and possibly an "uncontrolled non-valuable exercise of authority" from a person, place, and/or a thing that produces some type of restraint that causes an individual to either lose control of their objective and/or waiver the focus of a thought pattern that they once had, and/or become <u>mentally and emotionally imbalanced which can cause a spiritual disconnection from the third deity</u> that balances your "body, mind, and soul;" the soul which controls the emotional nature of a person by disabling the mind so that the heart can become emotionally effected, therefore producing stress, anger, worry, guilt, and/or the pain of depression. (Golden Rule No. 1)

We often allow these certain entities; in regards to people, places and/or things, especially if it is of no benefit to us.

Taking a look at something as simple as "love" for example. Love is supposed to be a combination of two individuals grafting themselves as one. Even the bible continuously illustrates the most effectiveness when a man and a woman become that team and not an act of a one-sided act of kindness.

Although love is in the eyes of both beholders, love can also be abused, singled-out, and/or manipulated into a hardship of consequences. Especially, if one catches on the controlling aspect of the relationship.

Yes I love you, and sure you can see your girlfriends at times, "but" just make sure that you're home whenever I call, okay?

Now within this same term; pertaining to the word "love," there are certain natures in which this word carries, also possesses "a tolerance level of endurance," and one of them is "patience."

Patience in the nature of love, although we try to unlimited our endurance with respect, we can also provide more harm to ourselves with the "hidden emotions of mental tolerations" to the extent that our very own point of pretending to extend our courteousness to an individual or individuals in order to reach the destiny provided, becomes a character of rudeness, demonstrated outwardly on our part.

Whether it is through the tone of our voice that seeps out, the body gestures of irritation, and/or the gazing into the dream world glance; because we have turned a death ear to not being attentive to the conversation when we have had just about had enough of all of what we could bare. Especially when "time" is involved.

And/or, the "limitation of time" that we thought and have pleaded about with a nervous sweat that we once had, has now became either robbed and/or altered. All because of whom we have become in contact and/or surrounded ourselves with, was given an unwelcome opportunity to control the conversations, the surroundings, the relationships, and/or the finances, as well as the timeline of our present future to be somewhere and/or reach a fulfillment of a responsibility, duty, and/or goal by the altering of our future through the "mishandling of control" in the present.

We're not talking about the mismanagement, but the mishandling of our very own authoritative control that somehow slipped away through our fingers without grasping that once we felt the situation, circumstance, criteria, and/or even addiction; if it relates to a person, place, or thing that keeps us from our objective, has become an uncomfortable state of recognition with its existence that causes an attitude adjustment, a mental and/or emotional realignment, and/or a psychological reality evaluation check that we are now faced with "unnecessary mind pressure."

Then there's people who we generally surround ourselves with that has this tendency to always present conversations of negativity. As they say, "negativity brings or presents more negativity." But the listener has a choice to either walk away, ignore the conversation, and/or better yet, just don't allow themselves to be drawn into the conversation.

The bible says in Proverb 13:20, "He that walketh with wise men shall be wise: but a companion of fools shall be destroyed." The bible also says in Proverb 18:21, "Death and life are in the power of the tongue: and they that love it shall eat the fruit thereof.

Basically, what we listen to is what we also could very well be feeding off of the fruits of its poisoned tree, once the tree, or shall we say, "the individual or individuals who carries the effected gossip and/or negative conversation disease," begins to affect us with a different view of focus.

Gossip, jokes, and/or tattletale's, false and/or true, are good example terms of how we can easily feed into it through the listening of information that was thrown out for any hearer to catch, as well as producing "negative mind clutter" to effect the focus of the listener.

"Control," depending on the mindset of the individual, can also be used as a "mechanism" [*mechanism - in reference to this golden rule, is any physical or mental process by which a result is produced - Webster's New World Dictionary*] by which one can produce the effects of paranoia to the opposite party with the pondering elements of curiosity, notions, speculations, and/or concerns to the effected party that was either drawn into, played-on; through verbal manipulating tactics, talked around, talked-over, talked about, and/or the exercise of a verbal control of power.

Generally, "authoritative control" maintains positive structure if used in its proper perspective. But often we find that the negative usage of authoritative control is about the domination of power over whatever entity that is present that could be subjected to being ruled over. The question is, "do we find ourselves becoming more mentally violated to the point that we cannot even speak up for ourselves, nor being apt to at least protest a debate, nor hold a conversation, in fear that we can become more intimidated by someone else's intellect and/or having a negative authoritative control over our lives?"

We should understand that time is valued and measured by what mechanism of control is being used, and how those among the negativity features; whether verbal abuse, conversational mutter, and/or the dominating actions of a person, place and/or thing can strip us, as well as rob us from where we were going, what we were supposed to be doing, and could there have been a better future for us, if we only looked from within and noticed that we ourselves did not take the consideration that we can create our own personal controlled environment through the "Accountability, Determination, and Commitment (ADC)" towards a better life than the life and the uncontrolled environment that we have subjected ourselves to.

- Be accountable for your own self-actions
- Be determined to take a positive step forward
- Be committed to be, do, and surround yourself with positivity, and learn to enjoy this beautiful lifestyle change

Here is a very easy example: You have a child and you would like to take that child to the park, but the park across the street from you is very trashy; empty liquor bottles tossed everywhere, little finger size plastic bags sitting on the swings, and paraphernalia lying all around.

Now there is a very clean park about two miles from where you live, would you go there in order to change into a more positive environment for you and your child, or would you settle for what's in front of your doorstep?

You do not have to subject yourself to a negative or uncontrolled environment, unless you choose to live in that manner. That also means including hanging around negative people, or those who want their control of glorification by bringing you down, and the ones that has nothing better to do with their time then to spend yours.

If you made it home from something that is negative, ask yourself what draws you back to it? Failure only exists if you stop trying to get back up again. And each time you get back up, you should already know the obstacle course that you have been continually facing.

Whether its poverty, addiction, or some type of abuse, it's about that time to overcome that obstacle, even if you need to acquire some type of assistance to help you.

As a reminder, have the courage like those whose pants hang below the butt in open public, or the ones who uses string as underwear. The only difference is that you are going to channel that courage and boldness in moving forward in life.

In all actuality, you could be struggling against yourself for nothing, and allowing "Mental Poverty" to consume you with shame.

WE ALREADY KNOW THE PAST, OBSERVE - NOT DWELL ON IT

Destiny *means* something to which a person or thing is destined [Destine is to direct, devise, or set apart for a specific purpose or place]. Destiny also means a predetermined course of events often held to be an irresistible power or agency.

Goal *means* the end toward which effort is directed: Aim.

[And "Aim" is to direct to or towards a specific object or goal.]

(Definitions taken from Webster's Ninth New Collegiate Dictionary)

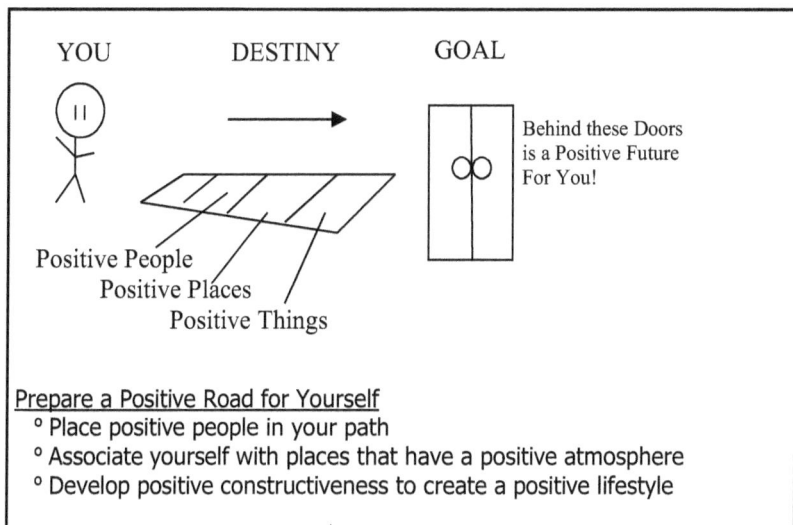

YOU　　　　DESTINY　　　GOAL

Behind these Doors
is a Positive Future
For You!

Positive People
Positive Places
Positive Things

Prepare a Positive Road for Yourself
° Place positive people in your path
° Associate yourself with places that have a positive atmosphere
° Develop positive constructiveness to create a positive lifestyle

A **"Puppet"** is one whose acts are controlled by an outside force or influence. [And "Influence" is to have an effect on the condition or development of; modify.]

NOTE: The definitions job to these paragraphs is to give a powerful meaning and purpose; into and onto, which these words are specifically directed. In this way, there can be more understandability that can be drawn out from within ourselves to direct our attention to the "self-actions" that we may be able to acknowledge within our different criteria's, turning those situations into learning tools to extract from and progress to a better dwelling [meaning to keep the attention directed] of our future.

Some people live their lives being manipulated to almost every voice of command and/or action. Then, there are those that manipulate others just to feel the power of control. Therefore, when we get into talking about "negative controlled environment" being similar to "uncontrolled environment," what we are looking at is the haphazard dangers of its effects towards self, others, places, and/or things.

I remember a time after coming out of an 11 years' worth of homelessness, pushing a shopping cart, begging and eating out of dumpsters on skidrow, when I finally got to see my mother before she passed away, I told her that I felt like I'm not succeeding in anything, that it has always been failure knocking on my door. She looked at me and grabbed both of my hands in comfort and said, **"Look at yourself now, you've reached your goal. Now it's time to work out your success!"** I never thought about it like that, I mean our initial goal is to come out of something that we have embedded ourselves into. Then, once we reached that goal no matter what it is, we are to work out our success from it. The same way is the term "Breakthrough". Anyone can have a major breakthrough, but can one maintain the success of it. Each golden rule is the working out the success through them. Making the commitment to God and yourself in the Covenant Pledge was exactly that, a breakthrough; committing to get your life back together and have positive control over it.

A good example is wanting to own a business - that is my goal. Once reached, it becomes how do I maintain it by working the kinks out of it – that's working out my success! Get it?! **Even by you reading this book, you're already stepping into a positive goal, you're getting back up!**

Let's have an 'After Question' Dialogue:

"After I read this book and I accidentally get in a situation again, what do I do?"

"Well, again, congratulations on this success of it."

"How do you figure?"

"Your subconscious mind immediately now realizes that you want to get back in control of your life again, or in this case, want to know what to do in order to regain back control. That's what a successful breakthrough does, giving you the ability to think in a positive way for yourself.

"Hum, I never thought about it like that."

"Yes, before you didn't know what to do. Now, your commitment to want to do better automatically induced the very first Golden Rule, which is "I need to take control of my life"."

"Okay, that sounds cool. So, what do I do next?"

"Brush yourself off and find out which Golden Rule itself applies to that particular moment in order to regain the self-awareness of the *how and what* not to do again, and move forward with a positive thinking solution to the problem [s] or poor choice [s] that was made."

"Thanks, now I understand about this successful breakthrough in which I can actually proclaim!"

-End Dialogue

BREAKTHROUGH – An important discovery, event, or development that helps to improve a situation or provide an answer to a problem. – Cambridge Dictionary

---

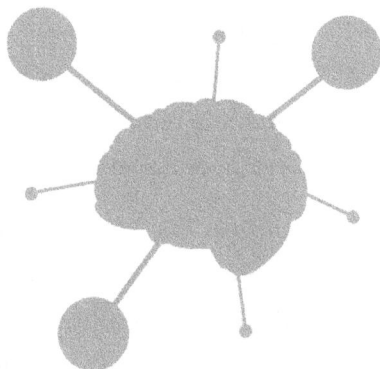

GOLDEN RULE 5

I will not take anymore "Mental Abuse", "Physical Abuse", and especially "Spiritual Abuse".

What is it that causes great confusion that a person can be used as a punching bag? Whether verbal and/or physical, people often feel that having that dominating spirit over someone or some-thing makes the masculinity of the individual, he/she or they, become more confident in their control. A better term would be "bully."

Even in religion, we often find some of those who were supposed to be servants; who claim to follow Christ actually abuse the gift of liberty to exercise submissiveness to one another. In this we call "spiritual abuse."

Now, spiritual abuse is a mental mind game played in the actions of certain religious individuals that usually claims their own level of how far one can submit, but instead places the weaker or less knowledgeable individuals in submission with harsh words, and/or the abuse of scriptures in order to manipulate for personal benefit and/or the recognition of authoritative gratitude.

Usually those who do not know the scriptures have a tendency to have the scriptures crammed down their throats in order to be obedient to those who went beyond the religion itself and have secretly placed themselves in a god-like position, but carries on with humanistic worldly flaws that in the fleshly sense they may not know or refuse to acknowledge, that what they may make someone eat might do them more harm than good.

That is what we consider taking mental abuse and trying to legalize its authenticity into a religious act, only to give reason and/or the consideration of oneself to become justified for their purpose and/or role in whatever level of ministerial position; including spouses, significant other, relatives, friends, etc., in a certain submissiveness of control that goes beyond the normal call of duty by misusing the Word of God get whatever one wants at that moment.

Example in the highest level: Badgering from across the pulpit with the exposure of confidential conversations that only certain parties are able to recognize.

Example in the lowest level: Making the spouse perform whatever is told from the bible (including the misuse of the scripture's terminology) in order to feel a sense of lordship and not companionship.

In which in any level of mental abuse; in the spiritual sense, is actually "crushing one's spirit" to please the appetite of the dominant in "verbal authoritative power." Therefore, did you know that "mental abuse" besides the explained aspects of spiritual abuse, can also produce another form of "physical abuse?" The harm of mental abuse is that it can induce symptoms which produces a mental illness beyond the tolerance level that a person could have endured, which it surpasses into a physical sickness that deteriorates the body. For example, "Depression."

Depression can cause an individual to do or perform things that he and/or she would not normally do. Like not eating or over eating, not sleeping or over sleeping, a decrease in motivation, an act of harm against themselves and/or other individuals, abnormal behavioral patterns, physical deterioration, a decrease in personal hygiene care, a participation in criminal acts, and/or negligent activities, over indulgence of normal drinking habits, taking up or excelling in addiction habits.

These things and similar as such, can also produce the physical destruction and/or the damaging to an individual's brain cells, as well as the internal organs.

In addition to having these types of symptoms, there can also be certain results that can formulate within any combination to the increase of deterioration of one's physical motor skills in order to perform mental and/or physical functions that they once normally had.

Apparently, physical abuse can also carry its destructive weight in the "external physical form" as well. In either terminology of "external" verses the "internal" form of physical abuse, the act of physical harm is still being brought upon an individual through by means of the individual's mental state of mind.

But the physical abuse that produces bodily harm from another need to be addressed and understood by the individual on the receiving end. The basic questionnaire is, "Why do a person need to be a physical slapping bag, a punching bag, a spit-on object, a kicking bag, and/or a slamming mat?" **Violence should never be condoned in any situation, circumstance, nor criteria.** But the individual must recognize that if their mental abuse has placed and/or positioned them into a mode to obtain physical abuse, they have allowed the "choice of freedom" to become consumed and replaced with the "regret of fear." In other words, "a person allowing themselves to be put in a position that holds a negative controlled environment."

Generally, individuals that doesn't remove themselves from a negative controlled environment is "stagnated." They feel that they cannot go anywhere, nor do anything without the permission of the controller. The controller who must feel a state of either being manipulative, jealous, inferior, and/or dominant, due to the lack of their own personal worth.

This is where "sanctuary" should be requested! The need to step away from false security that blinds the mind from and through mental abuse, and/or the physical violence that will produce the impact of a mental abuse criteria.

- The **First Sign**, is when a person cannot think for themselves.

- The **Second Sign**, is when an abused individual is starting to feel insignificant about themselves.

- The **Third Sign**, is when an individual is conned into believing that the physical abuse is only a "fluctuation period" in one's life.

- The **Fourth Sign**, is when an individual starts to accept self-endangerment when they lack the confidence of being able to get the help assistance that they need.

- The **Fifth Sign**, is simple. Losing the will power to survive, the notions of giving up, and/or the acknowledging of oneself as the abused weaker vessel.

And there is nothing more worse than the weaker vessel becoming surrounded by negative people; especially, when the controller has strategically placed his and/or her own band of "negative influential people" that continues a repetitious pattern of making the weaker vessel feel worthless about themselves.

What is progressing is a personal negative controlled environment which the controller has established. And once an individual can understand that the controller is the core to the negative controlled environment in his and/or her personal life, next it's about being able to remove oneself from the core problem. Then, we are back to finding and/or re-establishing sanctuary; or shall we say, "a safe haven."

You see, no-one should convince themselves that moving away from the problem produces more problems. Instead, the individual needs to get the assistance that they need, extract themselves from the situation, circumstance, and/or criteria with the proper guide of assistance that is available, as well as those that are specialized in individual and/or abusive family victim situations.

REMEMBER, ABUSE IS ABUSE!

No matter if it is performed in a religious context, a physical context, and/or in a mental context. God has given each and every individual "a free will" to choose their pathway in life, but Christ did not overcome the gates of hell only to see that his children is still living in the walls of bondage.

Hum…Let me get this straight. She is trapped in a relationship with a very bad man, and her only way of escape was to marry another man she only met two weeks ago? Well that band wagon has left. And wait till she gets home now. We all know what's going to happen next. Especially, since she was supposed to pay the rent and forgot.

Just how controlled can a person become before they realize that their life is now not their own?

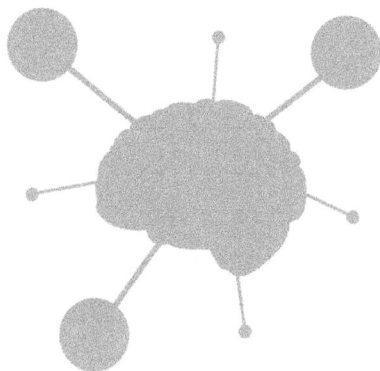

GOLDEN RULE 6

I will learn to think before I act.

One of the most important things that we must be able to learn is "knowing how to think." Of course, we all feel that we already know how to think and this would seem like a non-important factor because thinking should be a normal reaction within our daily lives. But truthfully, if how we react to situations is not projecting any form of a positive "thought out process of thinking" but causes down-slopes that places oneself to be surrounded by and/or with negativity, then the actions that one makes is lacking the ability of "Coherent Consciousness," by not being able to place together a positive thought process.

Rushing to take action if something is not in the right perspective is demonstrating "character failure" without first weighing the options of directions that this character failure might take us, especially if our "Christianic values" causes for one to be a primary example to the world. Meaning (*pertaining to the more religious aspects*) those who turned their life over to a more positive spiritual awakening at some point in their life, then breaching that spiritual oath with God or higher power by falling back into their old bad habits, *whether verbal or physical actions* without thinking it through. In which it may cause others to look at that individual now in a different light, and the respect that one once had begins to disintegrate and soon *over a period of time* remain on the opposite side of the tracks.

Our primary example to the world is the demonstrations of our actions. Our actions to the world carry the fruits of the third deity; the Holy Spirit. If our actions do not match up with these fruits, then not only will we be out of Christianic character, but spiritually disconnected as well.

These fruits that the bible talks about in Galatians 5:22 and 23 are "love, joy, peace, longsuffering, gentleness, goodness, faith, meekness, and temperance." But disregarding our Christianic values; according to a worldly way of living that drives our fleshly desires into trying to satisfy the immoralities [*lewd behaviors*] in Galatians 5:19-21, our character could either pick up and/or continue in "adultery, fornication, uncleanness, lasciviousness (lust - an unnatural desire), idolatry, witchcraft, hatred, variance (a difference in attitude; argumentative), emulations (trying to compete against), wrath, strife, seditions (rebellious), heresies (an opinion or belief contradicting established religious teachings or authority), envying, murders, drunkenness, revellings (wild uncontrolled parties), and such a like."

And if you noticed, these are "bad action results" which also gathers its own "negative controlled environments" that will also take a person through hell and back, just by not making the right choices of a direction of decisions that could have been prevented.

Are there times that your thinking gets you a traffic ticket, jail time, probation status, marital situations, forfeit of a place to rest your head, the missing of meals which causes hunger days and possibly an unscheduled fast, the status of living day by day, unnecessary conflicts with neighbors, friends, relatives, and/or even on a jobsite, and/or hospital time? How about if you are in or going to become involved in ministry, and it becomes unstable? Well, this is either "risk thinking" and/or an "unwarranted process of control" that are based upon repeated actions that finally came to a halt and/or have become an uncontrollable falling domino stack that fell a different direction then you anticipated for not applying a positive thought-out process in understanding the consequences if you choose to follow through with inexcusable actions. Especially, if there is no dire emergency to accept the results.

Therefore, "to act, is to behave." Then do our actions perform in a manner that causes us to try to withdrawal from the mistakes that we have put into motion without first thinking about the consequences, the direction of additional actions, and/or the destiny that it will take us, let alone a possibility to take us away from our goal?

Here is a scenario that will be taken from a scene which came from the movie "What's the Worst that Could Happen?" with actor Martin Lawrence:

"In the beginning of the movie, there was a young woman at an auction gallery auctioning off her father's painting in order to receive some funding to pay for the hotel bill. So apparently, she is receiving a limited credit line by going in debt with this expensive hotel in which she is presently trying to continue to stay. Although Martin Lawrence was sitting next to her, sweet talking in her ear, he doesn't buy the painting for her, instead the painting got sold for the amount of two thousand five hundred dollars. Now, we're talking about a young woman who has a degree in anthropology and is looking for a job since her previous internet career adventure had crashed. But now she is displayed, according to the next few scenes of the movie, lounging in her bed reading a book. Then, taking a few scenes back, Martin Lawrence decides to steal the painting from the buyer and then brings the painting to her lavished hotel suite, and afterwards she decides to stay with him. Later down a scene he gets her a job at his uncle's establishment, but his uncle is also a criminal as well."

###

What we have to look at is, "What was her intended focus at the beginning, what type of thinking was she doing, what type of environment she was jumping in and out of, and/or is there, or could there have been any type of "personal controlled environment at anytime?"

Remember, this all has to begin and end with the way an individual will think, is thinking, then having the completed thought-out process and the type of execution one decides upon.

The answer should bring solutions that could have been done to avoid "negative fallouts," or shall we say, "negative aftermath." Meaning that what was a quick fix and/or a temporary fix in the beginning, ended up with more problems and/or damages to repair in the long run.

And if you thought that she was "Risk Thinking," you are probably right! For one, although she was in a positive frame of mind, she did not weigh the differences between an expensive hotel verses a cheap hotel with a longer period of stay. And within this, it could have bought her more amble time to continue searching for a job. This would have given her "her own personal controlled environment," because she would be in control of her situation.

But, although there was no indication that she managed a "personal controlled environment," her "risk thinking" placed her into an "uncontrolled environment," an environment that is unstable and/or unpredictable. Then she also has allowed herself to become acquainted with a "negative controlled environment," because these individuals that she is now involved in, are in the profession of criminal activities.

Therefore, we can also put our actions in a risk-taking state of mind. Even if our intentions started off positive, we need to create a complete picture; a blueprint, just as simple as starting with you as the "core", then by placing an outer circle around your core and drawing a bunch of little circles on the line of the outer circle of your core, and just start placing the names of people, places, and/or things that you generally affiliate yourself with by placing a (+) sign for 'positive influence', or a (-) sign for 'negative influence', and see what kind of personal environment you have unintentionally or unknowingly created for yourself.

Try it on the next page!

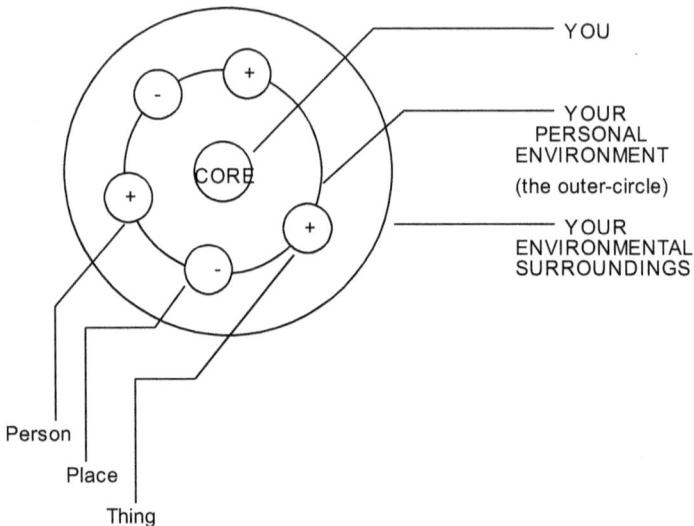

YOU

YOUR
PERSONAL
ENVIRONMENT
(the outer-circle)

YOUR
ENVIRONMENTAL
SURROUNDINGS

CORE

Person

Place

Thing

Create Your Blueprint from Scratch

You will then find it pretty interesting to see the way or range in the amount of positivity summing up next to the way or range in the amount of negativity that creates an "influential" environment that could or have fluctuated your future and/or your lifestyle.

So, in order to better ourselves from the position that we are currently in or going to be involved in, we need to formulate a "positive personal controlled environment" that are/and will be logically connected and intelligibly linked to other "positive controlled environments."

• Now each negative that is on your outer circle, how many of them have their own negative and/or uncontrolled environment?

- If they do, then draw an outer circle for each individualized negative core that happens to be attached to your outer circle.

- If it is a person, is the person negative or is the person surrounded by a negative environment? Or is the person the controller of a negative environment?

- If it is a place or a thing, then is it an uncontrolled environment or is it a negative controlled environment?

Even such as this simple blue print level of learning about our personal environment, it does reflect on whether we have personal control of our very own surroundings. Also, it detects the flow of positivity and negativity that we can draw unto ourselves without really discovering the existence of its reality.

If the person is surrounded by a negative controlled environment, it doesn't necessarily mean that the individual is negative.

Take the mental, physical, and spiritual abusive relationships for example, the individual could be controlled in someone else's negative controlled environment and/or in an "uncontrolled environment" that they have subjected themselves into, but is involved with you in your personal environment with a lot of negativity attached. (Golden Rule No. 5)

Even if it is 'an involvement concerning a relationship,' each individual has to have their own personal controlled environment in order to survive as a team unto God, meaning the two becoming one under the same roof without trying to become a controller over the other with different environmental backgrounds. Introducing or forcing the other into a world that is neither healthy nor positive against his or her wishes is reflecting a dominating presence.

If such a case may arise, pertaining to one person having to depart from the other with the obtaining of a positive personal controlled environment, one does not have to depart into another negative or unstable environment. And rests assure as the bible holds truth, one does not have the authority from God to over-rule their mate.

The bible says, in 1st Corinthian 7:3, "Let the husband render due benevolence: and likewise also the wife unto the husband." [*Benevolence means for both individuals to treat each other with acts of kindness, as well as doing good to one another.*]

And speaking towards the men, "although we are supposed to be the head of the family, it doesn't necessarily mean that we are lord over them. Because the bible does say, in 1st Peter 3:7, "Likewise, ye husbands, dwell with them according to knowledge, giving honour unto the wife, as unto the weaker vessel, as being heirs together of the grace of life; that your prayers be not hindered."

But we could go another direction too, and that is, "But if the unbelieving depart, let him depart. A brother or a sister is not under bondage in such cases: [bondage meaning, slavery, captivity, entrapment, including abusive relationships] but God has called us to peace." 1st Corinthians 7:15

Well, you're probably thinking, what if I am a believer and married to an abusive believer? Then just remember this, if you tried everything else; prayer, mental and/or spiritual assistance, whatever positive it took to keep the glue in the relationship and the believer still refuses to stop the abuse, then that believer is undertowed with some serious issues because in Ephesians 5:25-28 states that the husband is to love his wife as he would love himself. So, if he is enslaving you into bondage with mental, physical, and/or spiritual abuse, then he is in reality enslaving himself or falsifying his own belief. God will in fact not hold you responsible for leaving him, and visa-versa.

"Till death do us part" does not mean, 'I will deal with the abuse until I no longer have a mind of my own, and my fate is now in the hands of the abuser to control until I die.' No, in this case it means, 'if we can <u>no longer have a purpose to be together</u>, then it is time to depart' because staying together (including companion or significant other) for obligation or codependency reasons and not love, is a very bad accident waiting to happen in abusiveness.

Death does not have to be until one's life has ceased from this world; it can also mean the ending of the union between the two parties involved.

Thus, the environment of both parties is supposed to be positive, or at least becoming more positive affiliated when joining together! But if one's personal environment is very negative, then we see why relationships do not last. They do not or have not, nor discovered not, or refused the acknowledgement of not removing the negativity that spills into another human beings' life and/or lifestyle.

So negativity can also be brought on by means of relatives as well as friends, and even the unwarranted introduction of people who you come to be in contact with that was already in an uncontrolled or negative controlled environment as well.

But you can start introducing repair into their life and/or lifestyle if you want them to be a positive influence in your personal environment by giving them a book of their own about "Coherent Consciousness," so they can also develop their own positive personal controlled environment, and so on, and so forth.

Now remember, "All the cores (a person, a place, and/or a thing) that controls a negative controlled environment" needs to be extracted from your life. Basically, by either leaving them alone and/or removing yourself away from it/them. But you still have to 'think before you act' to keep from leaping into another situation without positioning positive connectors to self.

And, even in relationships, an individual's personal controlled environment should always have a professional counselor; spiritual or general community assistance on hand. In that way, if there is ever a problem or situation that cannot be handled, they can help you with it. This also protects and reinforces your outer circle when two personal environments become connected as one.

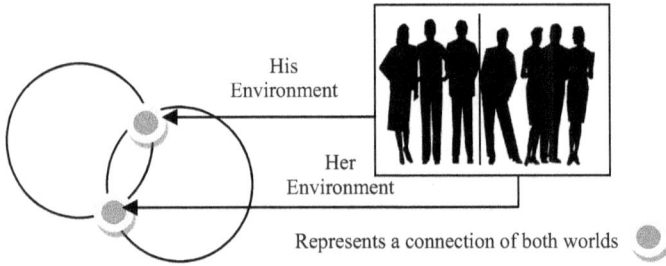

His Environment

Her Environment

Represents a connection of both worlds

A friend walked into my office one day and reminded me of a movie called *Trading Places* with Eddie Murphy and Dan Aykroyd. In this movie, Eddie was a homeless bum trying to make a buck in the streets. The Duke brothers, Randolph and Mortimer creates this lifestyle exchange experiment between the two men and places a $1 dollar bet to see if who would adapt to their new environment. What was interesting when it comes to "*to act, is to behave*", is the fact that when Eddie, now in wealth, threw a wild party with all types of down and out walks of life from the streets, he pauses for a moment and then begin to think things out; he realizes that he doesn't have to accept this type of environment or way of life again. Instead, he makes his first attempt to better himself by getting all the rift rafts out of his home, pushing away the Draculas' that has only one purpose in mind, and that is to suck the life out of someone or zombify a person with a sense of control. He eventually, over a period of time, pushes forward and learns the business of brokerage and excels it with his street knowledge, but in a positive way.

In other words, you can change the direction of your life or fate by not acting the way you use to behave, whether it is a negative verbal and/or physical behavioral pattern that kept you a distance from the positive elements in life.

Unless we have a job as clowns, we should stop acting like unpaid fools and think what we're about to do and say, because again, the meaning of 'act' *is to behave.*

When we often read something out of the bible like Galatians 5:19-21, we generally visually skim at the presents of the word[s] on paper rather than looking into its meaning. The "power of the tongue" is also powerful, even when we silently speak of a word [s] in thought without the verbal tone. This can also mean that we can receive a conviction within and contain its source of power by ignoring truth within itself, and with one's relationship with God. Therefore, our outward appearance would become more plastic and noticeable when we continually disregard the Christianic way of life that we asked for and came to know. Not the jumping, shouting, and the attending of sermons, but the way of life that shows love and compassion, as well as refraining or abstaining oneself from forbidden fruits that causes mental or physical harm also.

But remember this, a conviction can only function within oneself if there is something that needs to be (1) addressed, (2) hidden, and/or (3) rectified. The "free-will to choose" is always left in the hands of the beholder, only if the beholder so chooses to exercise that power of freedom in order to bring **"Redemption Power"** into one's life. Knowing and recognizing that there is a problem is far better than ignoring it or convincing (fooling) yourself that it will be better the next day, week, or month.

A person has a choice to either continue to be a **"sinner"** (*or one who sins out of stupidity*) who is still being saved by grace; until grace runs out, or a **"saint"** (*or someone who is thinking in the right direction*) moving onto perfection where an individual will learn not to continue repeating the same mistakes in order for a grace period to become reactivated again, so that the individual will have amble time in God's perspective. But also, to return from the sinful actions on which one has forced God's hand to keep oneself from evil spiritual entities that preys on the disobedient in Christ, and manifests its demonic self into our earthly world to promote a kill, steal, and destroy effect to one's testimony [s] on how he, she or they were enlightened in the first place.

In other words, how a person came to know God, and how many excuses will God take before God says, "No more, because I thought that my grace was sufficient enough for you until you took advantage of it."

The Repeater's Story

Here is an example of someone who keeps a bible, believes in its strength, and prays to God that if he was to ever get in a jam again to help bail him out. Note: Repeaters and those that are getting abused can understand this story with a clear thought.

Example: There was this man comfortable in his own home until he hears a car pulling up in his driveway, and soon after there was this knock at the door. He answered it. The person at the door warned him of a flood that was coming and that he needed to vacate the area, or he will die. The man said, "Okay, thank you, . . . God will save me," and went back into finishing whatever he was doing to get comfortable again. The flood came and began to rise. Then there was this loud tap on the window, and he went to see what was going on. He opened the window and there sat this person in a boat yelling, "Get in! If you don't you will surely die!" The man said, "That's okay, God will save me," and closed the window. A few hours later, you see that this man is now sitting on the top of the roof. A helicopter flew over and saw the man sitting on the roof and dropped a rope-type ladder. The person in the helicopter said, "Hey mister, we're here to help you, grab ahold and climb up." The man, now standing on his roof, soon to be ankle knee-deep in water looks up and bellows out, "Naw, that's okay, thanks. You go on, God will save me." The helicopter pulled the rope-type ladder back up and left.

It doesn't matter how good of a floater one may think he or she can be, sooner or later that individual will soon drown into the deepest problems of their life while asking for help but won't 'think' (*process in their noodle*) to act upon it. The man drowns and went to heaven earlier than scheduled. He asked, "God, I thought you would save me?" God says, "I tried to, but either you were too stubborn or some 'thing' that you are personally dealing with held you back from taking notice of the help that was right in front of you. I sent a car, the boat, and the helicopter, and yet you still refuse or ignored the assistance that I provided for you."

The comfort that may ease your situation temporarily at that moment may be the one thing that keeps you from seeing things for what they really are in your life.

But I will share you this as it was told to me. "There is a difference between brainwashing and mind-control. Brainwashing is an enemy who applies some type of torture over a period of time until that is all you know and accept. Mind-control comes from a person that you think you can trust, but in reality have you doing or performing things (cloaking); like one thing leading to another, and you find yourself wondering how you ended up here."

EVEN IN BUSINESS . . .

We can bite off more than we can chew. A business without positive structure is a business that was built on the sand. There is also the case where we place friendship over business and the friendship is one-sided. That means, if I accept the consequences of losing the benefits that is due mine over a friendship [*Friendship includes: relationships, relatives, friends, co-workers, and even some form of addictive entity [s], etc.*] [*Benefits includes: owning a business, or working for a business, having a salary, earning some type of wages, etc.,*] that doesn't have a positive justification, especially if what I consider to be my friend but in reality I have fixated on something that doesn't exist, then my future is enslaved by my own demise. The entity will soon depart, but my memory will remain stagnated in negativity because I allowed myself to be fooled by a codependency action that the entity was worth more than the success of my future.

Here's something else to remember: If no one has a stake (claim; something to lose or gain) in your business or personal life, but provide "odd" suggestions or advise on how you should operate your business or run your home other than those of a profession with credibility, be very cautious – don't accept anything someone or advertising gimmick might say or display. Take notes before agreeing, and before taking some form of action that may alter your personal environment and/or create some mental instability. Don't turn yourself into a victim of misfortunate circumstances. Some do mean well, but there are others who just runs off the mouth just to impress or have audible control. If things go sour, the individual can just walk away, leaving you holding a grocery bag full of problems.

A Short Self-Internal Checkup:

- How many golden rules have you read so far?
- Can you recall any of their meanings?
- Are you still committed to having a positive control over your life?
- Do you still want a positive lifestyle?
- Do you know how to get back into the book to find the area to succeed in your breakthrough if you need to?
- Sometimes it is helpful to read your Covenant Pledge again to know that you are somebody in God! Can you do that for yourself every now-and-then?
- Now that wasn't that hard, was it?

Remember: If you ever feel frustrated over something, always remember Golden Rule No. 1 "I need to take control of my life!"

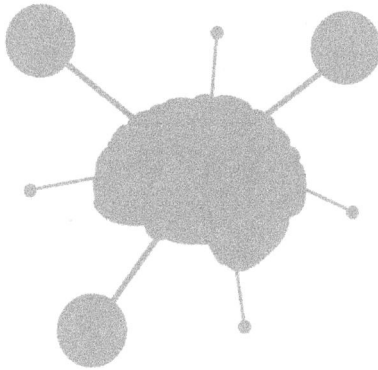

GOLDEN RULE 7

I will learn to think before I speak.

There are times when we start and/or continue to speak; speaking in terms of a manner of irritation, we have either over expressed our own conversation, provided unnecessary information that was or was not intended, voiced opinions that could be harmful to the hearer and/or to ourselves, and/or did not perform a positive reaction to a negative word or words that reverses our "Neutral or Positive Thinking" into "Risk Thinking" actions [Golden Rule No. 6] by promoting a negative environment that can become violent or promote more abusiveness [Golden Rule No. 5] and/or more negativity that produces "an Earthly Manifested Destructive Personal Collision" with a person, place, and/or thing from a spiritual manifestation of a negative force that we cannot see, but can be naturally felt through a mental unguarded disposition and/or the physical movement of actions that can even cause a financial backlash, if a lack of our discerning of a spiritual battle is starting to brew if and/or when we become disconnected with the information feeder [the Holy Spirit], from the spiritual realm itself which depends upon the tones, the gestures, the types of words that we use, combine and/or create, that have given authoritative command words into the hands of unclean spirits (or people, places, or things we have no business being there or associated with) to give them the green light to perform chaos into our personal environment, in which we actually brought this upon ourselves by not performing "Positive thinking" into the situation, circumstance, and/or criteria that is at hand.

The bible says in Proverb 29:11, "A fool uttered all his mind: but a wise man keepeth it in till afterwards."

There are also scriptures like:

- Whoso keepeth his mouth and his tongue keepeth his soul from troubles. Proverb 21:23

- Speak not into the ears of a fool: for he will despise the wisdom of thy words. Proverb 23:9

- Seeth thou a man that is hasty in his words? There is more hope of a fool than of him. Proverb 29:20

Also, that what we speak out could have authoritative power to put something in motion like the bible says in Proverb 18:21, that "Death and life are in the power of the tongue: and they that love it shall eat the fruit thereof."

Now concerning "Neutral Thinking," neutral thinking can cause "Risk thinking" if an individual is not cautious of what is being said and/or what is about to flow out from the individual's mouth at the time when an intended or unintended feedback [reply] is requested, and/or not requested.

"Neutral Thinking" is generally a wondering of thought or an area of thought that hasn't been processed. But a spontaneous answer without knowledge ability of what was said is "Not Considered Positive Thinking" unless there were previous experiences from the past that could or can be utilized in a positive constructive manner or the equation of an understandability that can formulate positive structure within the thinking process, provided if the statement was heard with attentiveness.

Therefore, then this would be considered "Positive Thinking" before a verbal statement and/or physical actions of gestures are attached (*meaning adding a verbal or physical action to the statement or question given*) can be completely processed and released through a positive "Thought Out" process to the individual or individuals in whom the giving out of a response is release to.

Can you feel the vibe in this picture?

- What type of environment do you see?
- Is there only one or multiple environments?
- Can you guess who's doing what?

Yeah, I thought she knew better than to talk among gossipers. She even said things in her testimony that I'm trying to avoid thinking about. But hey, I'm just going to stay over here and mind my own business and get out this parking lot. This is a weekday, and bible study has now been over two hours ago.

?

Chatter Chatter Chatter

1 2 3 4 5 6 7

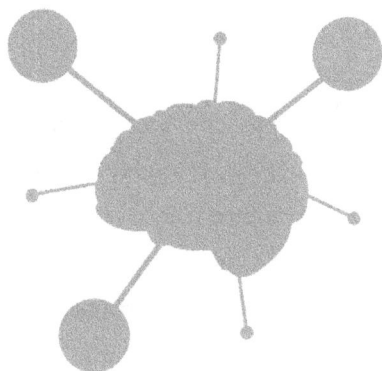

GOLDEN RULE 8

I will learn to think before I do.

One of the hardest things to learn in life is the chances that we take when we do something without first analyzing [*examining in detail of*] the situation, circumstance, or criteria that effects our personal being, our personal environment, and/or our environmental surroundings.

For example, like "doing something that we shouldn't be doing and not being able to explain ourselves for doing it." But please, don't use Golden Rule No. 2 as an excuse to not give an explanation for wrong doing and/or doing something out of impulse, or better yet, producing more "yes's" than more "no's" because of a friendship that could have "negative effect influences," a relationship that deals with mental pressure and/or future abuse [*abuse meaning at any level* (Golden Rule No. 5)], a job and/or career, or being in a situation, or being under a circumstance or within a certain criteria, and/or even a promiscuous promotions [*getting yourself involved in of all sorts of things and people*] for a one-time event that can bar, entrap, and/or enslave you mentally, as well as; depending on the situation, physically. And if you are being spiritually enslaved into doing something, then you are still involving the "mind process" of not being able to use positive thinking.

Just remember that God will not place charge over your life to do things that would be in conflict with the fruits of the Spirit. The only conflict with the Spirit is if you know that the Spirit of the Lord which is inside of you is receiving the pressure of disconnection, each time your "yes" keeps gaining control over His "no." And that the promotion (*going forth into doing something*) to whom and/or what you applied yourself into performing caused you to obtain a "negative characteristic" about yourself, and causing you to become easily controlled and/or hypnotically willed to do things outside of your character.

This is "negatively fashioning" ourselves to become more of an action "yes" person, and/or grooming ourselves "without thought," as a pose [*to set oneself up*] to become or becoming "people pleasers."

In understanding that this is not "positive thinking" nor a "positive thought out process," especially when the mental pressure of deciding whether or not that to perform some type of task becomes more vague [*not clearly defined, grasped, or* understood- *Webster's Dictionary*], and the word "yes" becomes more frequent. Even to the point that its meaning doesn't become verbally impressive anymore, but the actions whether good or bad, starts to speak louder in the performance itself.

Don't let "co-dependency" become another focal point of just "doing," but to understand that if there is a caution to be considered, rethink about the situation, circumstance, and/or criteria that you would allow yourself to be involved into and/or led to be involved with.

> Co-dependency can also be an addition that is so bad, that you become more comfortable having someone or some 'thing' control the thinking for you. And the worst part is that you cannot survive without the feeling of being controlled.

That is why it is so important for you to have your own "personal positive controlled environment," even if involved in a relationship. Both parties can produce positivity together and with each other independently. In other words, positive co-dependency can be healthy only if it doesn't involve having to not having a voice or opinion of your own.

Generally, if both worlds; yours and someone else's personal environment comes into contact, your positive structure of your "positive environmental surroundings" will uplift, strengthen, and compel you to maintain "positive characteristics" in your "positive personal controlled environment that will gain more positive authority in regulating what is and should be positive in "Your World."

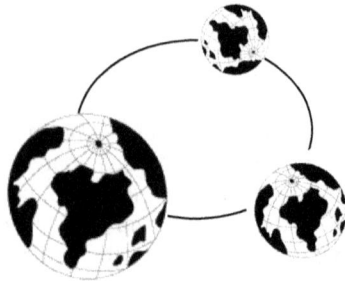

Inside your world:

- You as a Positive Core

- Your Positive Personal Controlled Environment

- And Your Positive Environmental Surroundings or the Positive Environmental Surroundings that you involved yourself with, as well as for your family, relatives, and friends, places and things that you so choose to enter into your "Positive Personal Controlled Environment."

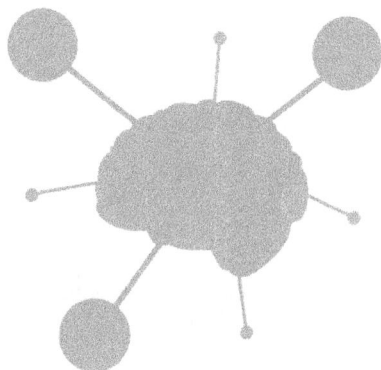

GOLDEN RULE 9

For my "New Life" awaits me!

I remember in the old Christian days of my youth, I was always told to be thankful for what I have. And as I grown older, I entered into a career field with beautiful benefits that involves the maintaining of military and commercial aircrafts. Yet still, I stuck with the value of this mentality, is to be thankful for what I have. And even though I lost everything, became strung out and homeless, as long as there was food supplied into the dumpsters, and poverty assistance places to go to eat, I have now become 'accustomed' to being thankful for what I have.

Almost 11 years have passed, and I'm still strung out and living in a cardboard box. Instead of being thankful for what I have, I am beginning to convince myself, that this is all that I am.

- There are individuals that are constantly being told to be thankful for what they have. Whether it is the roof over their heads, the clothes on their backs, and/or the food that's in their belly.

- There are individuals that are also in mental, spiritual, and/or physical abusive situations, and are convincing themselves, that not only to be thankful, but this is all that they are.

But suppose <u>you can excel and still be thankful for what you have.</u> Remember, although I have eaten poverty food at a poverty level, my mind is still in a poverty mode. Therefore, if I'm still thanking God for what I have, is that where God is limiting me to become of?

In the course of time, I went to several different churches, poverty dressed as far as the poverty state of mind will allow me to dress, <u>finding my backwards motions to end up repeatedly rededicating my life to Christ over and over again.</u> Even though blessed with a job from pushing a shopping cart in the homeless community, to pushing several shopping carts at a supermarket, I am still limited, because <u>I allowed my mind to become limited.</u> I got all cleaned up and became all spiritual, and even spoke in tongues; even though I didn't allow myself to be forced by the "spiritual abuse" at some religious events. You know, the ones that believe it comes from the diaphragm of your belly, therefore when your belly is pressed like a button, up pops the activated voice of the Holy Spirit. But, above all else, my mind is still in the stagnation to excel. And although I am grateful for what I now have, I have not yet understood, nor discovered, that I have "a personal environment that needs restructuring," as well as not knowing what it is like to have a "positive control" over it.

The bible tells us that we can practically pray for a better future then the one we have now. Although it is truly a blessing to thank God for what we have, but stagnating ourselves into believing that God cannot give to us a "Higher Standard in Life" with humility, is "negative thinking" from positive people.

That's like thanking God for the limited ability to prosper, and that what a person has is better than nothing. But if any of us have ever experienced "the nothing," then within ourselves, we should be able to detect that there must be more to us and/or our future; while here on this earth than what we are led to believe.

Then one day, we will eventually; if we have not already done so, arise one morning, and even or perhaps when the day has ended, begin to feel that this is all that I am. (A void in our heart that makes us not complete or content within ourselves). Especially, when our personal environment is fluctuating in a negative fashion and/or that we do not have control over it, as well as the environmental surroundings that could have some negative effects that is violating our personal environment.

Then, if you have been exposed to scriptures of prosperity, been preached at about prosperity, as well as Children of God being able to have a higher standard about themselves, even when you felt Gods presents to inform you that you are supposed to be in a different position of life itself then the one that troubles the manifestation of heavenly blessings, then it is the "New Life" in this world that is still awaiting "You!"

Repeat this phrase as many times as needed:

"My New Life Still Awaits Me!"

And listen to the heart of your thinking and the sound of your voice. If there is no excitement, enthusiasm, then find the Golden Rule that you are struggling with and mentally learn to stand by its general principles; *the golden rule itself.*

Most times we're afraid of what lies ahead if we take a plunge into wanting to better ourselves. The real problem is that there is either some 'thing' or someone, or perhaps your own self, not allowing you to act upon what's best for you, but instead allow you to continue "play dreaming" of a future that you continue to wish for.

Let it sink in because we do have a tendency to forget what we were brought out of repeatedly, and now have the opportunity with these 9 Golden Rules to have control over our own lives. Time to be productive and make positive use of it with a positive state of mind for another successful breakthrough. Brush yourself off and let's go better ourselves!

An Epilogue to the Golden Rules

Deuteronomy 8:11-20

New International Version (NIV)

[11] Be careful that you do not forget the LORD your God, failing to observe his commands, his laws and his decrees that I am giving you this day. [12] Otherwise, when you eat and are satisfied, when you build fine houses and settle down, [13] and when your herds and flocks grow large and your silver and gold increase and all you have is multiplied, [14] then your heart will become proud and you will forget the LORD your God, who brought you out of Egypt, out of the land of slavery. [15] He led you through the vast and dreadful wilderness, that thirsty and waterless land, with its venomous snakes and scorpions. He brought you water out of hard rock. [16] He gave you manna to eat in the wilderness, something your ancestors had never known, to humble and test you so that in the end it might go well with you. [17] You may say to yourself, "My power and the strength of my hands have produced this wealth for me." [18] But remember the LORD your God, for it is he who gives

you the ability to produce wealth, and so confirms his covenant, which he swore to your ancestors, as it is today.

¹⁹ If you ever forget the LORD your God and follow other gods and worship and bow down to them, I testify against you today that you will surely be destroyed. ²⁰ Like the nations the LORD destroyed before you, so you will be destroyed for not obeying the LORD your God.

The moral of the story is:

You can be self-sufficient *without forgetting God*. Learn to take control of your life and just simply give credit, a simple "thank you" for watching your back when you were in an out of a bad controlled situation (whether it's a person, place, or thing), and didn't know what to do.

Don't be afraid to tell someone that is positive:
"I'm In the Transition of My New Life!"

HOW TO GET MY "NEW LIFE" IN GEAR
LEARNING MY ROAD MAP

In mapping out your world, you must first understand the three basic elements that make up your world.

- The **"Core"** is you. You are the center part of your own very being in existence. Whether by choice or not, you have the ability to make a difference in the future direction on the way you want to live your life.

- Your **Personal Environment.** It is the surrounding atmosphere of what and who you have 'personally' associated yourself to. It is healthier and more beneficial to examine yourself in determining if someone or some 'thing' in your life can be a hindrance towards a better future for yourself and/or your family.

- Your **Environmental Surroundings.** Your surroundings is the area on which you now live in and the community on which you believe that you might have to adjust to. Again, whether by choice or not, if the area is not productive to your being able to excel, then mentally, you should only look at it as a 'temporary stay' and not as though you are in bondage to that location. You just have to set yourself a positive mentality and create a logical goal (strategy) on how to exit your Egypt, even if you have to disconnect yourself from others, especially those who place depression type reminders of your finances, or your former addictions, or circumstances that they claim is beyond your control.

When I lost everything I had and became homeless on skidrow, I soon realized that I connected myself with those that threw 'hope' away, along with bathing, the changing into cleaner clothes, the loss of consciousness to beg, the self-esteem and the dignity of just being human.

These people are not losers, they're lost and forgot their way back, and most of the time there is always someone or some 'thing' that is more convincing enough to make sure that a person cannot exercise their mind to want to move forward from the position that that person is currently in.

After 11 years of being tormented to the illusional fact that I am supposed to be part of this lost community, I began to accept *confusion* verses *illusion* that 'why am I still out here,' especially if I accepted God into my life way back when. Now years later, I realized that God has given me a free will to choose, and the simplest form of choosing was all mental; the choice between positive thinking and the 'being lost' condition of negative thinking.

Once I started learning how to extract myself from the negativity that I connected myself to, my thinking became more clear, and the confidence within myself that I can move forward in life became a lot stronger.

To remove myself from being a repeater in any situation, circumstance, and criteria, I needed to be devoted to myself on how to better my life and have a better lifestyle than I was accustomed to. I needed a simple and yet an effective vow; a pledge that reminds me, to myself and God, that I will use my noodle (my mind), so I can be at a positive ease with new or freshly restored joy in my heart the way God intended.

HOW TO GET STARTED ON THAT ROAD
(Bookmark your pages to gain easy access.)

The First thing I did is to recite my personal covenant pledge from time to time.

✓ It's on Page 3.

The Second thing is reading keywords to help me identify the way that I am thinking and understanding the environment that I'm in at certain times.

✓ They're on Page 90.

The Third thing was to memorize the 9 Golden Rules that activates a positive and determined way of thinking.

✓ They're listed on Page 9.

The Fourth thing is follow the directions of the Blueprints on how to make my road to a successful breakthrough a permanent one.

✓ The Blueprints start on Page 92.

Do not fool ourselves into thinking this is an overnight process. It took patience, understanding, and the memorization of those 9 Golden Rules.

READING MY KEYWORDS TO SUCCESSFUL LIVING

- **Coherent Consciousness-** Being able to place together a positive thought process.

- **Discernment-** Is the ability to perceive or recognize clearly.

- **Positive Thinking-** Is the ability to discern a constructive thought process.

- **Negative Thinking-** Is the processing of destructive thought patterns.

- **Risk Thinking-** Is a thought-out process of chance. Whether good or bad, it is an exposure of how oneself places their outcome.

- **Mental Poverty-** Is the inability to make or discern positive thinking, which produces poor choices that are based upon our feelings and our emotions. Mental poverty is the combination of distractions and discouragements. The more the distractions and the more of the discouragements that you obtain, then it becomes the more of poor choices that you will make.

- **Environment-** An area of surroundings; along with its conditions that one might place themselves in.

- **Controlled Environment-** Is an environment that is regulated and/or in an authoritative power by a person, place, or thing.

- **Uncontrolled Environment-** Is an environment that is either hazardous, destructive, and/or wayward [meaning unpredictable].

- **Negative Controlled Environment-** Is an environment that is controlled in a negative functioning pattern.

- **Positive Controlled Environment-** Is a controlled environment that produces constructive developments.

- **Personal Controlled Environment-** Is the ability of an individual to authoritate and/or regulate the control of his or her own surroundings.

- **Core-** Is the central part, center of focus, and/or starting point of anything that is either reliable and/or responsible for the activity, growth, depletion, development, and/or the destruction of itself, and/or its surroundings; depending upon the make-up of the surrounding structure in which it is contained in, and/or surrounded by.

BLUEPRINT - Stage 1 Discovering

You are the "Core".
Everything at this point begins with understanding yourself.

- ✓ *Remember, this book is a guide to help you with your independence to have a positive future.*
- ✓ *Don't be afraid to admit to yourself about things concerning the below questions that makes you aware of the conditions that you are in and facing.*
- ✓ *It's about how the world you are now living in is set up, and how to reconstruct those conditions to a better future and positive lifestyle.*

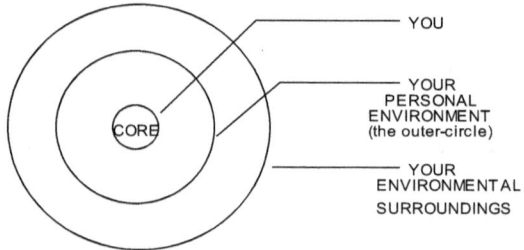

YOU

YOUR PERSONAL ENVIRONMENT (the outer-circle)

CORE

YOUR ENVIRONMENTAL SURROUNDINGS

1st How do you appear to yourself, "Negative" or "Positive?"

2nd Do you know how you appear to others? In a Negative or Positive fashion?

3rd Do you have a "Positive Friend" in Your "Personal Environment," that can honestly tell you abou yourself?

4th Did you know, that you have a "Personal Environment?"

5th Did you know, that you can have "Positive Control" over your Personal Environment?"

6th Did you know that you can "Restructure Your Outer-Circle with Positive People, Places and Th

7th Is your "Environmental Surroundings," Negative, Positive, or Uncontrolled (unpredictable)?

8th Did you know that you can "Create Your Own Positive Controlled Environmental Surroundings Outside Of A Negative Environment," if you cannot move away from it?

NOTES OF - Stage 1 Discovering

BLUEPRINT - Stage 2 Identifying

It's your "Personal Environment".
✓ *Create your own world on a piece of paper with the three elements.*
✓ *Next, place little worlds around your core.*
✓ *Replace the (+) with the positive entities you are associated with.*
✓ *Replace the (-) with the negative entities that you are associated with.*
✓ *If the negative entity[s] is a person, is that individual worth the effort on being blessed with a book? If not, disconnect yourself from that person, especially if they are 'content' with being negative. Remember, you're building your own positive world. Negative entities cannot help you or themselves succeed, period!*

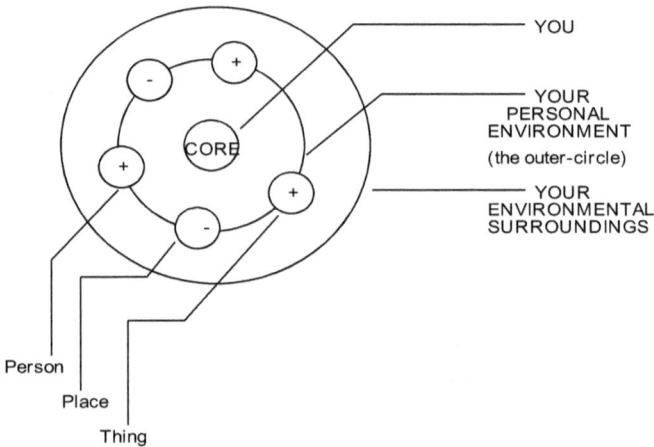

YOU

YOUR PERSONAL ENVIRONMENT
(the outer-circle)

YOUR ENVIRONMENTAL SURROUNDINGS

Person
Place
Thing

Did you know that your Personal Environment, is Your Outer-Circle that contains People, Places and Things.

Did you know that you can be influentially effected by the People, Places and Things that you surround yourself, without really even noticing your Mental and Emotional Change.

Did you know that each entity, carries a "Positive Influence" or a "Negative Influence."

Did you know that each entity has their own "Personal Environment."

Did you know that each entities environment, can effect your personal environment.

NOTES OF - Stage 2 Identifying

BLUEPRINT - Stage 3 **The Process of Restructure**

You need to be alert about other worlds that you connect with might carry negative baggage or skeletons.

✓ *It's time to acknowledge that who you associate with has their own world.*

✓ *If the positive entity[s] is a person (friend/relative), but is in a negative environment, make sure that the negative entities of their world do not filter into your world.*

✓ *If so, then you might have to <u>distance yourself</u> or let that person go because that person can bring a Dracula into your world without even realizing it.*

✓ *And if that person did know, then he or she is just 'zombified' (being controlled) in Dracula's world which is not good for you and the positive world that you're trying to build for yourself.*

Each Person has their own "Personal Environment" with an "Environmental Surrounding"

Is the Individual:
A Negative Person
A Positive Person
A Positive Person in a Negative Environment
A Controller

Is the Individual in a:
Negative Controlled Environment
Positive Controlled Environment
Uncontrolled Environment

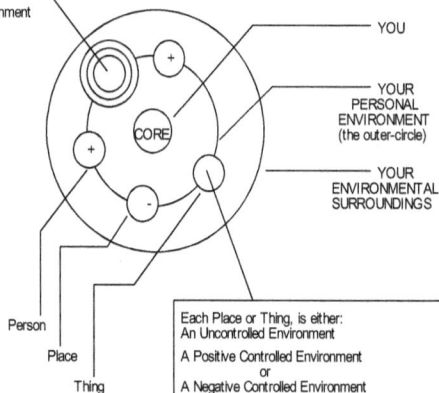

YOU

YOUR PERSONAL ENVIRONMENT (the outer-circle)

CORE

YOUR ENVIRONMENTAL SURROUNDINGS

Person

Place

Thing

Each Place or Thing, is either:
An Uncontrolled Environment
A Positive Controlled Environment
or
A Negative Controlled Environment

Each Place or Thing, can be Surrounded by:
A Positive Environmental Surrounding
or
A Negative Environmental Surrounding

NOTES OF - Stage 3 **The Process of Restructure**

BLUEPRINT - **Stage 4 Core Implosions**

Staying away from a core with
'Unpredictable Characteristics'.

✓ *You can now proudly say that "It is all about you!" It's you who is trying to better yourself, for you and/or your family.*
✓ *Don't associate with those that are continually unstable. You never know what their next wayward thinking may cost you and your future.*

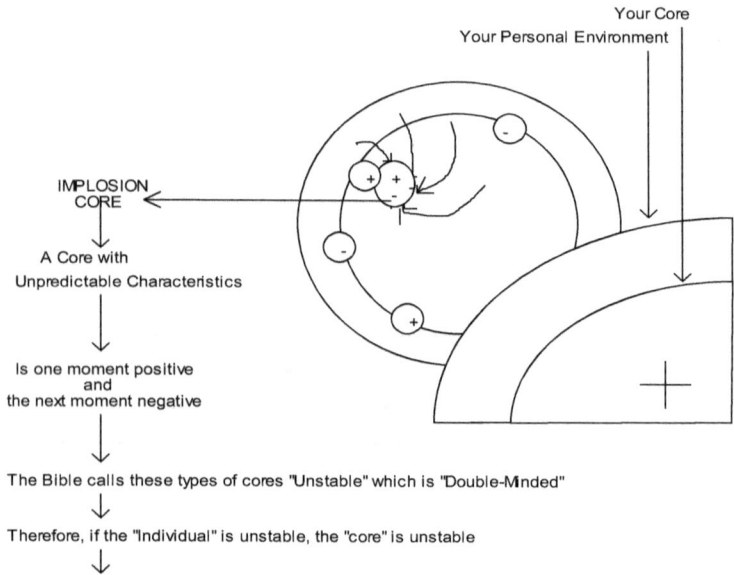

Your Core
Your Personal Environment

IMPLOSION
CORE

A Core with
Unpredictable Characteristics

Is one moment positive
and
the next moment negative

The Bible calls these types of cores "Unstable" which is "Double-Minded"

Therefore, if the "Individual" is unstable, the "core" is unstable

And if the core is unstable, there is "No Positive Controlled Personal Environment," but an "Implosion," that "Engulfs" [swallows up] other Personal Environments, and/or Environmental Surroundings, that he/she/they/it, tries to affiliate themselves with, by other cores not understanding and/or not discovering about their own personal environment, that this type of unstable core, that is swirling around on other cores "Outer-Circle," is capable of the damaging and/or the destruction of other cores and their personal environments, that are swirling around them, as well as the unstable core's own damages and/or the destruction of itself.

NOTES OF - Stage 4 Core Implosions

BLUEPRINT - Stage 5 Neutral Cores

Be careful when it comes to associating with those that goes through life without a care in the world.

✓ *It's not a good suggestion to associate with someone that can alter your objective to better yourself with someone that couldn't care less.*
✓ *But, you can be a 'positive influence' to someone by your actions and the way you now carry yourself. There's a difference between showing off and being an example.*
✓ *Remember: You're doing this for 'You', and not to impress someone.*

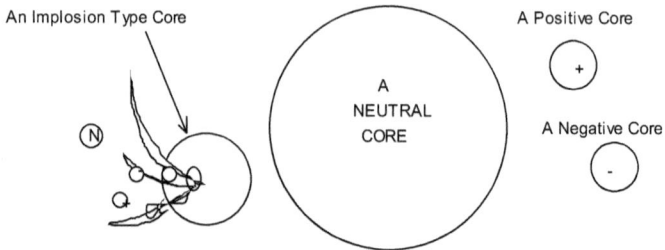

An Implosion Type Core

A Positive Core

A NEUTRAL CORE

A Negative Core

A "Neutral Core" is neither "Negative," nor "Positive"

But a Neutral Core can be "nurtured" and/or "swayed" to the "Strongest Energy (Influence)."

A neutral core is a core that remains dormant, until it allows another core to affiliate itself to the neutral core's outer-circle.

The core that attached itself to the outer-circle [personal environment] of the neutral core, has the ability to become a "Positive Influence," a "Negative Influence," or an "Implosion."

An Implosion, "Produces, Reproduces, Generates, and Regenerates" "Negative Cores."

In other words:

If a Neutral Core is engulfed, the outcome core is negative. (Produce)

If a Positive Core is engulfed, the outcome core is negative. (Generate)

If a Negative Core is engulfed, the outcome core is negative. (Reproduce or Regenerate)

But, a "Positive Core" may just have its environment effected, but is able to regroup, due to a "Positive Controlled Environment."

The more "Positivity" that a "Positive Core" collects for its "Personal Controlled Environment," the more control the core with have, in a deficiency in its outer-circle.

NOTES OF - Stage 5 Neutral Cores

My Breakthrough Cookies
Quotes written by the Author & Founder
© Steven Lawrence Hill Sr

Often times the simplest quote can provide stability for that moment.

1. In order to move forward in success, we have to look back and know what we have learned.

2. Challenging others is not a challenge, but challenging yourself to improve is the greatest of all.

3. My pockets are empty, but my mind keeps thinking. Sooner or later both will have to make a choice and agree on one thing, we need to learn from the experience that brought us to this point, in order to enjoy the fruits of life.

4. You do not have to go to the desert to notice that there is no water, but you do have to go in order to learn how to return back with groceries. For in the desert is where the successful see visions.

5. Consider being more humble than aggressive when it comes to obstacles trying to detour your success; because being humble can be the most aggressive move that allows you to think how that obstacle got there in the first place.

6. A little word of wisdom: Just because someone shares something, it doesn't mean that it is always true. And what makes truth becomes vague, is when multiple gossip overpowers it with a spread of false tales that can almost be undone. Thus, a seed has been planted with bad roots (origins). Easy example: Someone says that the sky is green, but it's not. But, by the time the false story returns, the sky is now purple. And yet the story started off false, therefore making a false story true.

7. If God didn't want you to be happy, he would not have created "Hope" to give you something to smile for.

8. Don't be disappointed in what you could not do, but discover what you did achieve or accomplished for that moment, and give yourself the praise...It's okay, God said that you are allowed to give yourself a pat-on-the-back once in a while when no-one else will, but just don't go overboard and forget who gave you that gracious moment.

9. Things don't always work out as planned. But the observation of its unraveling can create new options to explore and build on.

10. It is better to create a fine portrait, than just to slap paint on a canvas and call it art.

11. How you nurture your manuscript should be the same way as how you treat your child. For both are in your care, and it just depends on what type of parent you are to them in time.

12. When there is a storm in your life, you should learn to understand its reason for existence and prepare yourself, because the test is coming to see what experiences you have learned from it.

13. When there is another storm in your life, you should now be able to keep your head up in the midst of it, especially when the purpose of the storm is to strengthen whatever is lacking from the former test, in order to provide what is needed to build a *stronger-hold* to secure a better future for yourself.

14. The weather does not determine your business, it is you who decides the outcome of what is needed for that day.

15. Prosperity doesn't come cheap, especially if you do not wish to put forth the effort.

16. Goal setting is not to be looked at, but to be implemented.

17. Stress can destroy ambition, only if you cannot discern a way to remove the cause of its strength.

18. Complaining about a situation only digs a deeper hole for yourself, especially when you cannot think clearly on how to scale over the problem.

19. Starving yourself is no cure for success, but a lesson on what not to do.

20. Losing focus on the goal is more important now than it was when you first started goal-setting, because it takes your tunnel vision to succeed.

21. Success is not measured in dollars and cents; it is measured in the weight of wisdom that was triumphed through experience over a period of time.

22. If your faith in something is now in doubt, then doubt has robbed faith of its strength, and you of your glory.

23. I cannot prove myself worthy, for I have placed desires over need, chances over experience, and emotions over rationalization. Therefore, I must reverse the sails and salvage the vessel of my life.

24. Strength is a mindset of self-empowerment, induced by waves of encouragement. Thus, the heart still must be tamed in the adversities of life.

25. No one is ever free when they cannot approach the obstacle that limits them.

26. It takes years to become an overnight success. And an overnight success takes years to achieve its goal.

27. I shall look at the opportunity to study and then find ways to climb and overcome obstacles, and to never again sit up on its walls.

28. Mental freedom is surety for the opposite if one has the courage to move forward. In other words, some people have no idea that they can lock themselves as prisoners in their own mind simply by avoiding what needs to done or corrected in their lives until it is too late.

29. There's no free meal on the game of life unless you're willing to fool yourself and have blind sheep following your lead. And even then, sooner or later blind sheep will know when to walk away.

30. Some people need to be shoved forward in order to get their life straight. Just be careful how you push them, because there will always be two paths on the road, and one of them doesn't carry success.

31. Being an enabler is just as handicapped as the one who is enjoying the "fruits of spoils" of that individual. Wake up, splash water on your face, and look in the mirror again and you will see which one is aging quicker from the stress.

32. Don't handicap yourself at the starting gate when you know that there is always room for improvement.

33. Things cannot always be changed in the world around you, but you can make a positive difference in the ripple of life, especially your own.

34. Stepping out from the shadows of addictions, situations or circumstances doesn't mean that you're always bonded to its call in the distant future. It's okay hearing the dark whispers of its soul, just don't walk from the new light that you were given. For if you do,

you may not return and then you have learned nothing from its experience, nor the opportunity to carry the torch for others to see.

35. One step forward and two steps back can also be positive by examining the initial step and knowing what to look for the next time around.

36. Sometimes, all it takes is one spark to change the world.

Meet The
COHERENT CONSCIOUSNESS FOUNDER
I AM THE CAPTAIN OF MY VESSEL

CHRISTIAN MILLIONAIRE

Linked in.

I am the Captain of me. My vessel is my mind, a ship that God has given each of us to direct the physical and mental patterns of ourselves. Whether sane or mentally challenged, somewhere in thought, we understand certain avenues of "choice" that has been given within the boundaries of what liberty that we have obtained without restrictions; mentally. I've struggled with both; being schizophrenic and bi-polar my mind had been tormented to confusion while in the exterior I would appear normal. But one thing has been made quite clear within me, I wanted to do better than what I perceived what normal was for me. My mind has a gift for solutions, yet being challenged by everyday life, I somehow mentally derailed myself by the loss of hope, the dreams that others feel when they lose the value of self-esteem. But because of my gifted ability as a philosopher; one who studies the basic principles in the knowledge of thought and the nature of a universal expression of truism, *meaning* - considering the obvious truth of matters, my mind would map out a pathway to want to succeed better than the (former) present state of depression. I am what would be considered as a "Savant." A mental health nurse who explained to me what I am, which is describing 'individuals with a developmental disorder with one or more areas of expertise, that has an ability or brilliance.' You can view some of my credentials on Linkedin under ASA Publishing Corporation. My other credentials *other than* being a Christian minister and a life coach, at times makes me wonder more about my various abilities, and if I can be a blessing by utilizing this gift to help others in the most despairing moments of their lives.

When I first introduced "Mental Poverty," in Monroe Community Mental Health in Monroe, Michigan, then at another health center in Detroit, they both were astound by something that was never thought of within mental blueprints; a development that my mind had mapped out about its meaning of 'making poor choices'. I became a founder of a mental solution format and was requested for brief introductory seminars on my discovery "Coherent Consciousness". My mother and I accepted this newfound untapped discovery as a gift from God. Through all the tragedies in my life, this is my purpose, not the credentials itself, but the experiences that propelled me to understand how to get up, brush myself off and move forward in a positive way, and explain the solutions on how I did it.

The Golden Rules of a Successful Breakthrough is what I considered an inspiration of God. Yes, I am a Christian, but I am also a Child of God that believes that God is a Universal God; one who does not pick and choose a denomination, but places religion as the aspect of love, the giving of oneself to others in a time of need, and not become worldly hung over by eating any ole doctrine that leads people into chaotic confusion or negative pathways that promotes spiritual blindness as to pushes one so deep behind the mindset, that depression creates a circumstance that forces one's mind into believing that '*this is all that I am*' and '*codependency is my avenue to succeed, for without this I am nothing*'. This is all a derailment of the mind or the controlling element of some 'thing' that places our "freedom of choice" for positive thinking in bondage. This means that our ship is sailing a straggly course over a waterfall.

My purpose that God had given me is to help you turn your ship in the right direction and set a course for positive thinking, and obtain a positive successful breakthrough.

"I Shall look at the opportunity to study and then find ways to climb and overcome obstacles, and to never again sit up on its walls."
©Steven Lawrence Hill Sr.

DON'T PLAY DREAM, LET'S DO SOMETHING ABOUT IT!

The one thing I would like for you to do, is to remind yourself of the positivity things that you will be doing, and having a positive lifestyle that you are going to become accustomed to. It's your time, your world; a positive world that you can create for yourself. Now, the next following pages will be for you to start taking pictures of your beginning positive world. As you grow more and more into positivity, or shall I say that positivity will start gravitating toward you, remove the old pictures, date and store them away and begin replacing them back in this book with new updated pictures, and so-on. It will be like looking at yourself in the mirror and watching your transformation and conversion from your old self, and into the new you. *Observe your own successful breakthrough!*

What's so cool about it, is that it's even scriptural (*below*) where everything you have just learned about Coherent Consciousness, has been rolled up into one biblical summary. Check it out and go live your positive lifestyle!

---EPHESIANS 4:17-32 (NIV)---

So I tell you this, and insist on it in the Lord, that you must no longer live as the Gentiles do, in the futility of their thinking. They are darkened in their understanding and separated from the life of God because of the ignorance that is in them due to the hardening of their hearts. Having lost all sensitivity, they have given themselves over to sensuality so as to indulge in every kind of impurity, and they are full of greed. That, however, is not the way of life you learned when you heard about Christ and were taught in him in accordance with the truth that is in Jesus. You were taught, with regard to your former way of life, to <u>put off your old self, which is being corrupted by its deceitful desires; to be made new in the attitude of your minds; and to put on the new self</u>, created to be like God in true righteousness and holiness.

Therefore, each of you must put off falsehood and speak truthfully to your neighbor, for we are all members of one body. "In your anger do not sin": Do not let the sun go down while you are still angry, and do not give the devil a foothold. Anyone who has been stealing must steal no longer, but must work, doing something useful with their own hands, that they may have something to share with those in need. <u>Do not let any unwholesome talk come out of your mouths, but only what is helpful for building others up according to their needs, that it may benefit those who listen. And do not grieve the Holy Spirit of God, with whom you were sealed for the day of redemption.</u> Get rid of all bitterness, rage and anger, brawling and slander, along with every form of malice. Be kind and compassionate to one another, forgiving each other, just as in Christ

God forgave you.

In case you want to get assistance
You Should Know for Knowledge Purposes

AMHCA
American Mental Health Counselors Association
2000 Revision

Code of Ethics

PRINCIPLE 1 Welfare of the Consumer
E) **Diversity**

1. Mental health counselors do not condone or engage in any discrimination based on age, color, culture, disability, ethnic group, gender, race, religion, sexual orientation, marital status or socioeconomic status.

2. Mental health counselors will actively attempt to understand the diverse cultural backgrounds of the clients with whom they work. This includes learning how the counselor's own cultural/ethical/racial/religious identity impacts his or her own values and beliefs about the counseling process. When there is a conflict between the client's goals, identity and/or values and those of the mental health counselor, a referral to an appropriate colleague must be arranged.

Create a Mini Book Collage
OBSERVE MY NEW CHANGEOVER
TAKE A PICTURE OF YOU DOING SOMETHING
POSITIVE
Staple or paperclip it here.

TAKE A PICTURE OF A POSITIVE PLACE TO HANG OUT

Staple or paperclip it here.

TAKE A PICTURE OF THE NEW YOU
Staple or paperclip it here.

TAKE A PICTURE OF SOMETHING THAT YOU CAN BE PROUD OF

Staple or paperclip it here.

www.ingramcontent.com/pod-product-compliance
Lightning Source LLC
Chambersburg PA
CBHW071352090426
42738CB00012B/3088